The Jewish Festivals and Jesus Christ

John Sungchul Hong

EMETH PRESS
www.emethpress.com

The Jewish Festivals and Jesus Christ

Copyright © 2012 John Sungchul Hong
Printed in the United States of America on acid-free paper

All rights reserved. No part of this book may be reproduced, or stored in a retrieval system or transmitted in any form or by any means, electronic, mechanical, photocopying, recording, scanning or otherwise, except as permitted by the 1976 United States Copyright Act, or with the prior written permission of Emeth Press. Requests for permission should be addressed to: Emeth Press, P. O. Box 23961, Lexington, KY 40523-3961.   http://www.emethpress.com.

Library of Congress Cataloging-in-Publication Data

Hong, Sung Chul.
  The Jewish festivals and Jesus Christ / John Sungchul Hong.
     p. cm.
  Includes index.
  ISBN 978-1-60947-029-6 (alk. paper)
  1. Fasts and feasts in the Bible--Typology. 2. Bible. O.T. Leviticus XXIII--Criticism, interpretation, etc. 3. Bible. N.T.--Relation to the Old Testament. 4. Bible. O.T.--Relation to the New Testament. I. Title.
  BS680.F37H66 2012
  222'.13064--dc23
                              2012011734

Front Cover
Replica of the Temple menorah, made by The Temple Institute, 12/11/2007. Author is Ariely (used by permission), The menorah is the seven-branched ancient lampstand made of gold and used in the portable sanctuary set up by Moses in the wilderness and later in the Temple in Jerusalem. Fresh olive oil of the purest quality was burned daily to light its lamps.

Contents

Foreword / 5

Preface / 7

Introduction / 11

    1. The Festivals / 17

    2. Sabbath / 25

    3. The Passover / 39

    4. Passover and Jesus / 51

    5. The Unleavened Bread / 63

    6. The First Fruits / 75

    7. Waiting for Pentecost / 87

    8. The Pentecost / 97

    9. The Trumpets / 111

    10. The Day of Atonement / 126

    11. The Tabernacles / 141

Conclusion / 155

Index / 163

Foreword

Unfortunately many Christians are largely ignorant of the Old Testament roots of their New Testament faith. Although they give lip service to the inspiration of the Old Testament, and carry a Bible, three quarters of which is devoted to the Old Testament, they rarely read it, and almost never study it. The result of this ignorance is often tragic, because the New Testament writers were all steeped in the Old Testament and answered Old Testament questions. Thus, readers who do not know the Old Testament can very easily misinterpret the New Testament. The most serious of these misinterpretations is the modern one that explains salvation as merely involving the forgiveness of sins and the assurance of eternal life, which is not the case at all. As a rudimentary study of the Old Testament makes clear, salvation involves an ongoing walk with God, in which the believer is continually transformed into the likeness of the character of God.

Another existing error that must be avoided is the suggestion that the Old Testament should be understood without reference to the New. This suggestion implies that the New Testament writers who continually saw the work of Christ and the founding of the Church as the necessary fulfillment of the Old Testament, were doing something vaguely illegitimate by imposing connections that are not really there. Once again, such an attempt to divide the Testaments is disastrous. The Old Testament is a book that is incomplete by itself. By itself it is a book of failed hopes and broken dreams. Only when coupled to and read in the light of the New Testament does its true beauty and meaning become evident. In this coupling the hopes are realized and the dreams come true.

This book by Dr. John Hong makes a very valuable contribution toward correcting both of these errors. In it he helps the Christian believer understand what the Old Testament festivals have to do with Christian faith. This is an area that is especially poorly understood by many Christians. So the book helps to fill a very significant gap. Beginning with the spring festivals and moving through the year, Dr. Hong concludes his discussion with the final fall festival of Tabernacles. With each festival he explains what the Bible says about it, how it was observed in ancient times, how it is observed today, and what its significance is for Christian faith. In so doing, he shows how the stages of the Christian revelation, from the coming of Christ until the millennial reign of Christ, conform to the annual pattern of these festivals.

First presented in seminar form, then in serial form in the journal *Holiness*, they now reach their final form in this book. Because Dr. Hong is a preacher and evangelist as well as a writer, and because of the lengthy gestation period of the material, it comes to the reader in a well-matured and highly applicable form. Nothing here has not been thought through carefully and tested with a wide audience. While not everyone will agree with all of the eschatological positions taken, everyone can benefit from the way in which Dr. Hong shows that the Israelite festivals are important to the Christian not merely as historical background for his or her faith, but for the theological content they convey and for the way in which they illuminate the foundations of our faith. I commend Dr. Hong for this work.

John N. Oswalt, Ph.D.
Distinguished Professor of the Old Testament
Asbury Theological Seminary
Wilmore, KY, USA

Preface

Many Christians identify Leviticus as a difficult book. However, investigation reveals that no more interesting and systematic book exists than Leviticus. The better we understand and are familiar with the abundant contents and meaning of the book, the more we will know Leviticus as the precious Word of God. In particular, the teaching undulates deep and wide like a moving sea throughout Leviticus, with the message that we should be holy like the holy God.

In Leviticus, the methods to be holy like God are described in several ways. For example, the Israelites became holy by making offerings, by the selecting of their priests, by choosing the correct foods, by being different from the Gentiles at sexual practices, and by receiving the holy judgment when they were not being holy.

One more method of being holy was that of keeping festivals. The observation of festivals for the Israelites was as important a means of holiness as was keeping the law. Leviticus 23 describes the seven festivals required of the Israelites. While Exodus 23: 14-17 describes only three festivals, the proposal of the seven in Leviticus can be called the great expansion. Interestingly, while Numbers 28 and 29 deal with the seven festivals, Deuteronomy deals with only three.

While the three festivals in Exodus are proposed as dedications of holiness, the three festivals in Deuteronomy additionally emphasize the required need for a holy place of God's choosing. The descriptions of the seven festivals in Leviticus are from the priests' points of view, while those in Numbers are focused on the offerings that will be offered to God at each festival. Therefore, the four books of the Pentateuch complement one another in their descriptions of the festivals.

I have studied the seven festivals suggested in Leviticus. The book of Leviticus has given me great challenges along with immense inspiration. As I studied Leviticus, I became gradually fascinated by the contents and meaning. Ultimately, the seven festivals presented in the book became the final catch of fascination for me.

In particular, I was surprised at the fact that the seven festivals presented in Leviticus 23, as a whole, can be divided into three groups. The first three festivals—the Festival of Passover, the Festival of Unleavened Bread, and the Festival of the First Fruits—are the festivals of spring, and the last three festivals—the Festival of Trumpets, the Day of Atonement, and the Festival of Tabernacles—are the festivals of fall. The fact that the Festival of Pentecost is structurally placed between these two groups of festivals is noteworthy. In addition, the fact that all of the festivals have something to do with the seasons of agriculture was enough to attract me.

Additionally, uncovering the fact that the festivals are closely related to Christianity made me more interested in the seven of Leviticus. The three festivals of spring have already been fulfilled through the event of the cross of Jesus Christ, whereas the three festivals of fall are yet to be fulfilled by the Second Coming of Jesus Christ. Placed between the past and the future, the Festival of Pentecost bridges the gap between the festivals of spring and the festivals of fall, and thus bridges the gap between the First and Second Comings of Jesus Christ.

Whenever I teach Leviticus 23 I am repeatedly struck with awe. Every time, I feel the students are also inspired. In January of 2010, I delivered lectures to pastors at a seminar held at The World Evangelization Research Center. *Weolgan Seonggyeol* (*Monthly Holiness*), the official journal of the Jesus Korea Holiness Church also asked me to write about Leviticus 23. For these reasons, I have published what I have taught thus far.

While writing about the seven festivals in Leviticus 23, I realized two important points. The first was that my knowledge of the festivals was like that of being a little fish in a very big pond. By studying, I realized many new facts. For example, in fact, the festivals encompass so much information that each needs to become a book. Secondly, I realized the truth that the writer of the Bible is one, that is, God. The harmony between the Old Testament and the New became one of magnificent illumination.

Although the Israelites do not accept Jesus Christ as their Messiah, He is the protagonist of all festivals and the Law. The content of the Bible, whether reading about the Law or the festivals, is Jesus Christ. The truth is as Jesus Christ said: *You diligently study the Scriptures because you think that by them you possess eternal life. These are the Scriptures that testify about me* (John 5:39).

Even the disciples who followed Jesus could not believe that all Words of the Old Testament pointed to Jesus Christ. Therefore, we can acknowledge that to believe in Him was not easy for the Israelites. This aspect is proven by Jesus' saying to two disciples on the way to Emmaus: *How foolish you are, and how slow of heart to believe all that the prophets have spoken! ... And beginning with Moses and all the Prophets, he explained to them what was said in all the Scriptures concerning himself* (Luke 24:25, 27).

I can only thank the trustees of The World Evangelization Research Center who gave me a chance to more deeply study Leviticus 23, which I superficially knew before. I also deeply thank the editor and others of *Weolgan Seonggyeol* for helping me to publish the results of the study. I also thank Dr. John Oswalt, world-famous savant of the Old Testament at Asbury Theological Seminary, for writing a recommendation for me without any reservation.

However, above all, I glorify God, who unconditionally loves me; Jesus Christ, who saved me through the work of the redemption on the cross; and the Holy Spirit, who drew my attraction to Leviticus 23, through the work of illumination on my limited understanding, and who helps me to realize the indispensible, close relationship with Christianity that the festivals imply, and allows me to know Jesus Christ, our Savior, through the Word.

John Sungchul Hong
Sundo Kim Professor of Evangelism
Asbury Theological Seminary
Wilmore, KY 40390

Introduction

The Israelites at last put a period to their life of slavery that covered four hundred thirty years. They not only left an Egypt that suppressed them, but also began to proceed toward the land of promise, Canaan. The work of God above and the obedience of Moses below made their exodus possible. God of great power defeated Egypt for the Israelites, and Moses wisely led them by obeying God's guidance.

Of course, the ultimate goal of God's deliverance of the Israelites from Egypt was to lead them to Canaan (Deuteronomy 6:23). The will of God was not to simply physically lead them from Egypt. God wanted them to demonstrate His presence in Canaan. The reason was clear! They experienced God's love and power, but Gentiles they met along the way did not know such God. God's movement of the Israelites was a call to indirect evangelism.

However, God did not reserve this great call for only the Israelites. After having led them to Mount Sinai, God also gave them proper instruction and discipline in order for them to implement His call (Exodus 19:1; Numbers 10:10). The content of the discipline can be summarized as follows: first, receiving the law; second, building the tabernacle; and, third, learning the methods of sacrifice.

God's giving of the law to the Israelites is the first purpose of the Exodus. Giving the law allowed the Israelites, unlike the Gentiles, to resemble the attributes of God, as they lived in accordance with God's law (Exodus 19-24). The Exodus they experienced became a foundation for covenantal relationship with God through the law. The Israelites were able to demonstrate God to the Gentiles through this covenantal relationship.

Another great grace God bestowed upon the Israelites was His presence. How could such a holy God be upon human Israelites? For His coming, God made them build a tabernacle (Exodus 25-31). When they had built the tabernacle, God was upon the tabernacle as He had promised He would be (Exodus 25:22, 40:34-38).

This indwelling of God was truly a revolutionary and historical event. Since Adam and Eve disobeyed God, God intermittently presented Himself among human beings, but not consistently. The reason for interrupted visits was that the relationship between God and human beings had been broken. Nevertheless, God wanted to dwell in the people as He had when He first created them. The first time that the human mind realized the work of God occurred was when God's presence came to the tabernacle.

For now, the Israelites came to know **where** they were required to meet and worship God.

However, the following important question remained for them: *who and with what method can one go to God?* The book of Leviticus answers the question. Leviticus informed them on how to proceed to God. The methods were through sacrifice and the priest. The first method where God met human beings and where human beings went unto God was through sacrifice. Sacrifice consisted of various offerings (Leviticus 1-7). The second method was through a priest who brought the offerings before God (Leviticus 8-10). The Israelites could not bring an offering by themselves or proceed directly before God. For this reason they needed offerings to be sacrificed on their behalf. For example, a priest took an animal from an Israelite and then the priest presented the offering to God for the person. These two ways, sacrifice and the priest, allowed the Israelites to come closer to God.

Similarly, the Israelites, who had intimate relationships with God, had to demonstrate the relationship in their lives. The methods to demonstrate the relationship were two: cleanliness and holiness, about which Leviticus explains in detail. Cleanliness is described in Leviticus 11-16 and holiness in Leviticus 17-27, respectively. In summary, Leviticus deals with the problems of sin of the Israelites, which would appear to God (1-10), of cleanliness (11-16), and of holiness (17-27).

Since God is holy, the Israelites, who should represent Him, were required to be holy. The word *holiness* and its derivatives occur 152 times in Leviticus, mainly concentrated in chapters 17-27, suggesting in detail how the Israelites must live in holiness. Among the methods, Leviticus 23 teaches the Israelites to be holy by keeping the festivals. The purpose of this book is to study the festivals and explain their meaning.

The seven festivals appeared in Leviticus 23—Passover, the Festival of Unleavened Bread, the Festival of First Fruits, Pentecost, the Festival of Trumpets, the Day of Atonement, the Festival of Tabernacles (Booths)—are the fundamental law given to the Israelites. However, because all Scriptures are given by inspiration of the Holy Spirit, the law has the applied potential for transcending eras (2 Timothy 3:15, 2 Peter 1:21). On the one hand, these seven festivals are methods in order for the Israelites to live in holiness, and, on the other hand, they imply or suggest soteriology and eschatology, all essential to Christianity.

Therefore, this book attempts to investigate the historical background of the festivals, their practical application, their meaning to Christians, and the eschatological interpretation. After reading this book, readers will be familiar with the festivals in Leviticus 23, grasp the meaning that the festivals offer Christians, and as a result, act to be holy as did the Israelites. In order to be familiar with the festivals, above all, is to be familiar with Leviticus 23. A helpful introduction includes the following verses from the chapter:

> 1-2 The Lord said to Moses, Speak to the Israelites and say to them: These are my appointed festivals, the appointed festivals of the Lord, which you are to proclaim as sacred assemblies.

> 3 There are six days when you may work, but the seventh day is a Sabbath of rest, a day of sacred assembly. You are not to do any work; wherever you live, it is a Sabbath to the Lord.

> 4-5 These are the Lord's appointed festivals, the sacred assemblies you are to proclaim at their appointed times: The

Lord's Passover begins at twilight on the fourteenth day of the first month.

6-8 On the fifteenth day of that month the Lord's Festival of Unleavened Bread begins; for seven days you must eat bread made without yeast. On the first day hold a sacred assembly and do no regular work. For seven days present an offering made to the Lord by fire. And on the seventh day hold a sacred assembly and do no regular work.

9-14 The Lord said to Moses, Speak to the Israelites and say to them: When you enter the land I am going to give you and you reap its harvest, bring to the priest a sheaf of the first grain you harvest. He is to wave the sheaf before the Lord so it will be accepted on your behalf; the priest is to wave it on the day after the Sabbath. On the day you wave the sheaf, you must sacrifice as a burnt offering to the Lord a lamb a year old without defect, together with its grain offering of two-tenths of an ephah of fine flour mixed with oil—an offering made to the Lord by fire, a pleasing aroma—and its drink offering of a quarter of a hin of wine. You must not eat any bread, or roasted or new grain, until the very day you bring this offering to your God. This is to be a lasting ordinance for the generations to come, wherever you live.

15-22 From the day after the Sabbath, the day you brought the sheaf of the wave offering, count off seven full weeks. Count off fifty days up to the day after the seventh Sabbath, and then present an offering of new grain to the Lord. From wherever you live, bring two loaves made of two-tenths of an ephah of fine flour, baked with yeast, as a wave offering of First Fruits to the Lord. Present with this bread seven male lambs, each a year old and without defect, one young bull and two rams. They will be a burnt offering to the Lord, together with their grain offerings and drink offerings--an offering made by fire, an aroma pleasing to the Lord. Then sacrifice one male goat for a sin offering and two lambs, each a year old, for a fellowship offering. The priest is to wave the two lambs before the Lord as a wave offering, together with the bread of the First Fruits. They are a sacred offering to the Lord for the priest. On that same day you are to proclaim a sacred assembly and do no regular work. This is to be a lasting ordinance for the generations to come, wherever you live. When you reap the harvest of your land, do not reap to the very edges of your field or gather the gleanings of your harvest. Leave them for the poor and the alien. I am the Lord your God.

23-25 The Lord said to Moses, Say to the Israelites: On the first day of the seventh month you are to have a day of rest, a sacred assembly commemorated with trumpet blasts. Do no regular work, but present an offering made to the Lord by fire.

26-32 The Lord said to Moses, The tenth day of this seventh month is the Day of Atonement. Hold a sacred assembly and deny yourselves, and present an offering made to the Lord by fire. Do no work on that day, because it is the Day of Atonement, when atonement is made for you before the Lord your God. Anyone who does not deny himself on that day must be cut off from his people. I will destroy from among his people anyone who does any work on that day. You shall do no work at all. This is to be a lasting ordinance for the generations to come, wherever you live. It is a sabbath of rest for you, and you must deny yourselves. From the evening of the ninth day of the month until the following evening you are to observe your sabbath.

33-44 The Lord said to Moses, Say to the Israelites: On the fifteenth day of the seventh month the Lord's Festival of Tabernacles begins, and it lasts for seven days. The first day is a sacred assembly; do no regular work. For seven days present offerings made to the Lord by fire, and on the eighth day hold a sacred assembly and present an offering made to the Lord by fire. It is the closing assembly; do no regular work. (These are the Lord's appointed festivals, which you are to proclaim as sacred assemblies for bringing offerings made to the Lord by fire—the burnt offerings and grain offerings, sacrifices and drink offerings required for each day. These offerings are in addition to those for the Lord's Sabbaths and in addition to your gifts and whatever you have vowed and all the freewill offerings you give to the Lord.) So beginning with the fifteenth day of the seventh month, after you have gathered the crops of the land, celebrate the festival to the Lord for seven days; the first day is a day of rest, and the eighth day also is a day of rest. On the first day you are to take choice fruit from the trees, and palm fronds, leafy branches and poplars, and rejoice before the Lord your God for seven days. Celebrate this as a festival to the Lord for seven days each year. This is to be a lasting ordinance for the generations to come; celebrate it in the seventh month. Live in booths for seven days: All native-born Israelites are to live in booths so your descendants will know that I had the Israelites live in booths when I brought them out of Egypt. I am the Lord your God. So Moses announced to the Israelites the appointed festivals of the Lord (NIV: all Bible quotes are from NIV).

Chapter 1

The Festivals

The Word of God

According to God's Word in Leviticus 23:1-2, "The Lord said to Moses, Speak to the Israelites and say to them: These are my appointed festivals, the appointed festivals of the Lord, which you are to proclaim as sacred assemblies," we understand clearly that these festivals were given to the Israelites through Moses. As a result, the Israelites implemented these important festivals (Leviticus 23:9, 23, 26, 33).

The Israelites lived with the heavy burden of being free from sins every day and realized they were required to live clean and holy lives. However, God gave them an opportunity to regularly be free from such daily lives, which was the experience of "the festivals of Yahweh." Through the festivals, the Israelites received invigorating blessings and power from God. They also received the opportunity of festivals as a chance to renew their covenant with God.[1]

As mentioned above, the festivals were appointed occasions.[2] God enacted the date and rules for each. These festivals were also called sacred assemblies because God and human beings met for a holy purpose. Since the seven festivals of Yahweh presented in Leviticus 23 are holy assemblies for a holy purpose, the assemblies themselves are sacred and have rigid meanings. Understanding the reasons for the festivals is important.

---

1. Edward S. Gerstenberger, *Leviticus: A Commentary* (Louisville, KY: Westminster John Knox Press, 1996).

2. The festivals are called *moed* (דעומ) or plural *moadim* in Hebrew.

Importance of the Festivals

The first important reason for the festivals of Yahweh is that they are given to the Israelites, the special people who had the covenantal relationship with God. Through these festivals, the Israelites could come closer to God who gave them the covenant of grace. These festivals allowed the Israelites to attain rest away from daily life, reflect on the past, and enjoy the privilege of worshipping God.

The second reason for these festivals rests on their relationship with the agriculture of Israel. When these festivals were enacted, Israel was an agricultural society. After finishing harvest, the Israelites gathered together and reflected on the new year given to them. They thanked and worshipped God who gave them food from every harvest to prolong their lives. Their God was truly the God of life.

The third important reason allowed the Israelites to recollect the past. Regardless of age, sex, or economic status, these festivals were occasions to remember God who delivered the Israelites out of slavery. God did not forget the promise He had given their forefathers Abraham, Isaac, and Jacob. He saved them from Egypt with His tremendous love and power. The periods when the Israelites gathered, remembered, and praised such a God were the festivals of Yahweh.

The fourth important reason for Yahweh's seven festivals designates the redemptive ministry of Jesus Christ. Representatively, Passover, the first one of the seven festivals, clearly implied the redemptive death of Jesus Christ. Additionally, the Festival of Tabernacles, the last festival, pointed to the Second Advent of Christ. In the descriptive Scriptures of these two festivals we see the obvious suggestion that Jesus Christ will come again to the world in order to complete his redemptive ministry.

The festivals' fifth important reason deals with all people whom these festivals implicate. Of course, these festivals were initially given to the Israelites. However, if these festivals imply Jesus Christ, the Lord of the world, ultimately, they must be festivals for all human beings. The festivals teach that all Gentiles should also participate in the festivals and meet God, the Lord of the festivals. How are they to do this? Through Jesus Christ, of course.

The sixth important reason has to do with the occasion that each festival implies. Some festivals are related to spring, some to summer, and some to fall. This occurs because they are related to the agricultural seasons. However, to relate them to the Messiah Jesus Christ, the festivals include all the works He accomplished, including the past, the present, and the future.[3]

As a result, the seven festivals of Yahweh are not only for the Israelites, but for all human beings. They were festivals that included the past, as well as the present and the future. Jesus Christ, the Savior of the world, exists among all of the festivals. He stands in the midst of the time of the past, the present, and the future. For this reason, time in the Christian world was divided into B.C. and A.D. based on the axis of His birth. In other words, B.C. designates before His birth and A.D. after His birth.

Seven Festivals and Three Seasons

As mentioned earlier, the seven festivals that appear in Leviticus 23 are as follows: (1) Passover, (2) the Festival of Unleavened Bread, (3) the Festival of First Fruits, (4) Pentecost, (5) the Festival of Trumpets, (6) the Day of Atonement, and (7) the Festival of Tabernacles. A closer study reveals they are related to three seasons of agriculture. The first harvest of their year was barley, which correlates to the same time as Passover. The second harvest was wheat, which was the same time as Pentecost. The final harvest consisted of various fruits and products of field, which related to the same occasion as the Festival of Tabernacles.

So, are these three festivals—Passover, Pentecost, and the Festival of Tabernacles—the most important ones? In order to answer this question, Exodus 23:14-17 helps our understanding in its mentioning of the three festivals:

> Three times a year you are to celebrate a festival to me. Celebrate the Festival of Unleavened Bread; for seven days eat bread made without yeast, as I commanded you. Do this at the appointed time in the month of Abib, for in that month you came out of Egypt. No

---

3. To know more about the importance of the festivals, read the following book. Kevin Howard & Marvin Rosenthal, *The Festivals of the Lord* (Orlando, FL: Zion's Hope, Inc., 1997), 13-4.

one is to appear before me empty-handed. Celebrate the Festival of Harvest with the First Fruits of the crops you sow in your field. Celebrate the Festival of Ingathering at the end of the year, when you gather in your crops from the field. Three times a year all the men are to appear before the Sovereign Lord.

From the above we see that the Festival of Unleavened Bread engages with the Passover, and the Festival of Harvest with Pentecost. And the Festival of Ingathering is another expression for the Festival of Tabernacles.

The law that God gave to the Israelites includes three, not seven festivals as seen in Leviticus. That being the case, how can we best understand the difference and harmony between the three festivals in Exodus and the seven festivals in Leviticus? We need to study the agricultural seasons of Israel.

As mentioned earlier, three main agricultural seasons existed in Israel. First, according to the sacred calendar, the barley harvest is in January;[4] second, the wheat harvest is in March; and, third, the field harvest is in July. In January, Passover as well as the Festival of Unleavened Bread and the Festival of First Fruits occur together. In the sacred calendar of Israel, January corresponds to March and April in the solar calendar. Therefore, these three festivals are called the festivals of spring.

The second harvest, which is the wheat harvest, occurs in March on the sacred calendar, which corresponds to May and June on the solar calendar. Therefore, the wheat harvest or Pentecost is also called the festival of early summer.

The third harvest, or the fruit and field harvest, occurs in July according to the sacred calendar. Also in July, the Festival of Trumpets, the Day of Atonement, and the Festival of Tabernacles occur. The Festival of Trumpets and the Day of Atonement come before the Festival of Tabernacles. Since July on the sacred calendar of Israel corresponds to September and October on the solar calendar, these three festivals are also called the festivals of fall.

The following is an explanatory diagram:

---

4. In Israel, there are the sacred calendar in accordance with the event of redemption of God and the civil calendar in accordance with seasons. See below.

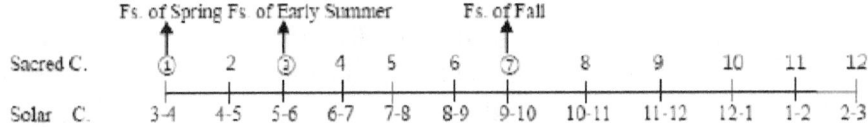

The three festivals recorded in Exodus and the seven in Leviticus are never contradictory. Simply speaking, while Exodus emphasizes three core festivals, Leviticus explains the three festivals and their following festivals in detail. The same three festivals given to the first generation that experienced the Exodus are also mentioned in Deuteronomy, within the law that was given to the second generation, right before the Israelites entered Canaan (Deuteronomy 16:1-17).

Two Kinds of Calendars of Israel

Now, let us explore why the New Year exists two times in Israel. As mentioned earlier, Israel has two New Years in accordance with the civil (solar) calendar and the sacred calendar. The beginning of the civil calendar is related to the creation of God. According to the Bible, New Year was started with the beginning of creation. For this reason, a New Year exists in accordance with the civil calendar, which was made based on the criterion of creation. And the New Year falls in the month of *Tishri*.[5] In Israel, another New Year also exists, which is based on what is called the sacred calendar. The reason is simple! The Israelites lived as slaves in Egypt for a long time and experienced liberation from Egypt by the grace of God. The liberation was impossible without the intervention of God. Calling the Israelites out of Egypt, God commanded them to enact that particular month as the first month (Exodus 12:2), which is the first month is the month of *Abib* and later on became known as *Nisan*, a Babylonian name.

The sacred calendar of Israel was the lunar calendar; the civil calendar was solar. On the solar calendar, a new day starts at mid-

---

5. Morris Epstein, *All about Jewish Holidays and Customs*, rev. ed. (Jersey city, NJ: KTAV Publishing House, 1970), 10.

night and lasts for twenty-four hours, but in the lunar calendar, a new day starts at sunset—around 6:00 P.M.—and lasts for twenty four hours. While the solar calendar is based on the numbers of days that the earth rotates the sun, the lunar calendar is based on the numbers of days that the moon rotates the earth. The moon's rotation of the earth takes 29.5 days, therefore if one multiplies 29.5 by twelve (months), the result is 354 days in a year.

In the sacred calendar of Israel, 11.25 days are fewer than in the solar calendar. In order to complement them, the Israelites cre- ated a leap month after December, that is, the month of **Adar**, one time per some years and called it **Adar Sheni** (the second month of Adar). They created a leap month for the third year, sixth year, eighth year, eleventh year, fourteenth year, seventeenth year, and the nineteenth year, using periods of nineteen years.[6]

Now, let us look at the names of the months and compare them to the solar calendar by using the following table[7]:

Divine Calendar	Folk Calendar	Babylonian Name	Canaan Name	Solar Calendar	Festival	Number of Day
1st Month	7th Month	Nisan (Neh. 2:1)	Month of Abib (Exo. 13:4)	March-April	Passover	30
2nd Month	8th Month	Iyar	Month of Zib (1 Kings 6:1)	April-May		29
3rd Month	9th Month	Sivan (Est. 8:9)		May-June	Festival of Weeks	30
4th Month	10th Month	Tamuz		June-July		29
5th Month	11th Month	Av		July-August		30
6th Month	12th Month	Elul (Neh. 6:15)		August-September		29
7th Month	1st Month	Tishri	Month of Ethanim (1 Kings 8:2)	September-October	Festival of Tabernacles	30
8th Month	2nd Month	Heshvan	Month of Bul (1 Kings 6:38)	October-November		20-30
9th Month	3rd Month	Kislev (Neh. 1:1)		November-December	festival of the Dedication	29-30
10th Month	4th Month	Tevet (Est. 2:16)		December-January		29
11th Month	5th Month	Shevat (Zec. 1:7)		January-February		30
12th Month	6th Month	Adar (Est. 3:7)		February-March	Festival of Purim	29-30

---

[6] Epstein, *All about Jewish Holidays and Customs*, 9.

7 .See http://www.timeemits.com/AoA_Articles/Jewish Calendar Sacred and Civil Years-gr.htm.

This basic knowledge of the month calendar of Israel may make it much easier to understand Jewish festivals. Frequent reference to the above calendar will be made during the following explanation of the festivals.

Chapter 2

Sabbath

Before He enacted festivals, God first mentioned the Sabbath in Leviticus 23:3: There are six days when you may work, but the seventh day is a Sabbath of rest, a day of sacred assembly. You are not to do any work; wherever you live, it is a Sabbath to the Lord. Notable here is that although God enacted the seven festivals for the first time, we find in Exodus 20:8-11 that He had already included the Sabbath in the Ten Commandments given on Mount Sinai. The Sabbath's distinguishing factors compared to the festivals become evident with further study.

Sabbath and the Festivals

When God enacted the festivals, why did He also mention Sabbath? What is the reason that Sabbath was first mentioned before mentioning the festivals? The idea seems somewhat unreasonable that Sabbath was introduced before the festivals.[1] According to the text, the festivals were not enacted until the Sabbath was mentioned (Leviticus 23: 4). Furthermore, while the festivals come one time per year, in keeping with the lunar calendar, Sabbath comes regardless of month, which makes Sabbath different from the festivals.

Therefore, what is the reason that the Sabbath is mentioned before and after the expression of the festivals of Yahweh? The answer is because although the Sabbath is not a festival, it is closely related to some of the festivals. Otherwise, no reason exists for the mentioning of the festivals of Yahweh before and after the Sabbath.

---

1. According to Leviticus 23:38, gifts, votive offerings, freewill offerings, and the Sabbath do not belong to the seven festivals. The Sabbath is *shabod* (תבש) in Hebrew.

In other words, after the festivals of Yahweh are introduced in Leviticus 23:2, the Sabbath is then introduced in verse 3; and in verse 4, the festivals of Yahweh are re-introduced.

What does the Sabbath have to do with the seven festivals/festivals? According to the text of Leviticus 23, the relationships are as follows: The first festival related to the Sabbath is the Festival of Unleavened Bread. In the enactment of the festival, God repeated the commandment in Leviticus 23:7: *On the first day hold a sacred assembly and do no regular work... on the seventh day hold a sacred assembly and do no regular work* (Leviticus 23:7-8). To reiterate: have a sacred assembly; do no laborious work; and rest!

The third and fourth festivals, the Festivals of First Fruits and Pentecost are indirectly related to the Sabbath. The reason is simple! The events of the festivals occur on the next day after a Sabbath, respectively. By elevating the First Fruits the priests present the offering *before the Lord for acceptance in your behalf...on the day after the Sabbath* (Leviticus 23:11). Additionally, the new-grain offering should also be presented on the next day after seven Sabbaths later (Leviticus 23: 15-16).

On the other hand, some festivals are directly related to the Sabbath. That the fifth festival, the Festival of Trumpets, on July 1st, should be unconditionally taken as a Sabbath is the solemn commandment of God (Leviticus 23:24). Additionally, for the sixth festival, the Day of Atonement (July 10th), the commandment of God is very clear: *You shall do no work at all... It is a Sabbath of rest for you, and you must deny yourselves. From the evening of the ninth day of the month until the following evening you are to observe your Sabbath* (Leviticus 23:31-32).

What is the relationship between the last festival, the Festival of Tabernacles, which starts on July 15th, and the Sabbath? Let us read to the Word of God: *On the first day shall be a holy convocation; you shall do no laborious work... on the eighth day you shall hold a holy convocation...it is a solemn assembly* (Leviticus 23:35-36). As a result, except for Passover, the remaining festivals relate to the Sabbath either directly, or indirectly. Therefore that the Sabbath is mentioned is naturally quite necessary.[2]

Enactment of the Sabbath

The beginning of the Sabbath comes from the fourth commandment of the Decalogue. Let us explore the Sabbath of the Decalogue that God gave to the people through Moses on Mount Sinai:

> Remember the Sabbath day by keeping it holy. Six days you shall labor and do all your work, but the seventh day is a Sabbath to the Lord your God. On it you shall not do any work, neither you, nor your son or daughter, nor your manservant or maidservant, nor your animals, nor the alien within your gates. For in six days the Lord made the heavens and the earth, the sea, and all that is in them, but he rested on the seventh day. Therefore the Lord blessed the Sabbath day and made it holy (Exodus 20:8-11).

The Israelites were not to work at all on the Sabbath, passively; and they were to also remember and observe the day as holy, actively. To rest with no labor is closely related to God's work of creation. God finished all, from light to human beings, during six days and rested on the seventh day. God blessed the day and made it holy (Genesis 2:2-3).

On that Sabbath day the Israelites should neither do any work, like God. They were to follow God. Such a fact had once before been emphasized in their life situation. When the Israelites were on the way to Mount Sinai they cried out to God for food, God gave them manna. They gathered manna every morning as their daily food. However, on the sixth day, God made them gather manna for two days and required they not do any work on the Sabbath (Exodus 16:22-26).

Finally, by including the Sabbath in the Decalogue, God enacted the day. As one of the commandments, the Sabbath played an important role in determining the way of life for the Israelites. As a

---

2. There is also an argument that the reason that the Sabbath first comes before the festivals is that all festivals was initiated from the Sabbath. For this, read the following book: Michael Mullins, *The Gospel of John, A commentary* (Co. Dublin, Ireland: The Columba Press, 2003), 165.

result, by enacting the Sabbath in relationship to God's own creation, He was requiring them to rest for a day after they had worked hard for six days. By doing so, they could obtain new energy in order to be creative in the coming new week.[3]

After the first generation experienced the Exodus, God again mentioned the importance of the Decalogue to the next generation before their entrance to the Promised Land of Canaan. The Sabbath's inclusion in the Decalogue was different to the new generation from the one related to the creation for the previous generation. To see a difference, let us review the commandment:

> Observe the Sabbath day by keeping it holy, as the Lord your God has commanded you. Six days you shall labor and do all your work, but the seventh day is a Sabbath to the Lord your God. On it you shall not do any work, neither you, nor your son or daughter, nor your manservant or maidservant, nor your ox, your donkey or any of your animals, nor the alien within your gates, so that your manservant and maidservant may rest, as you do. Remember that you were slaves in Egypt and that the Lord your God brought you out of there with a mighty hand and an outstretched arm. Therefore the Lord your God has commanded you to observe the Sabbath day (Deuteronomy 5:12-5).

The *regulations* of the Sabbath recorded in this passage are not different from those of the Sabbath given to the first generation in that they too should not work while remembering the day. However, a huge difference existed between the Sabbaths given the first generation and the second generation, which had to do with the *reason* for observing the Sabbath. The reason to rest on the Sabbath for the first generation dealt with the relationship with God's creation and rest. However, for the second generation the reason was different because God had saved the Israelites from Egypt. They had been slaves of Egypt for a long time. Liberation was totally impossible via only human power. The intervention of God was necessary, and at last, He intervened. God saved them "through a mighty hand and by an outstretched arm."

---

3. Gale A. Yee, *Jewish Festivals and the Gospel of John* (Wilmington, DA: Michael Glazier, 1989), 34.

As a result, God was the one who set aside a day per week. The God of Israel was not a mediocre god. He created not only all things, but also human beings. The Creator God commanded the Israelites to rest. Importantly, in addition, the Creator God was also the Redeemer God who redeemed the Israelites from Egypt. The God of redemption also commanded them to rest. These two were the amazing and highly significant works of God for the Israelites.

The Israelites had to set aside a day of each week to rest. To review, the reasons are two: the first relates to the creation work of God, and the other is because of the redemptive work of God. Of course, these two works are the works of God related to the salvation of human beings. Through creation, God initiated the history of salvation, and through the Exodus, He accomplished it. On the one hand, Israel should rest without work on the seventh day of a week, and, on the other hand, worship God, the Creator and Redeemer.[4]

Meaning of the Sabbath

Since the Sabbath is related to God's creation and redemption, its importance was sufficiently proved. Nevertheless, to study the meaning of the Sabbath more specifically as an indispensible element is important, because God asked the Israelites for three actions when He enacted the Sabbath. First, the Israelites should *make holy* the Sabbath. Second, they should *remember* the Sabbath. Third, they should *observe* the Sabbath.

To make the Sabbath holy means to set aside the day from the other days. Holiness is *kadosh* in Hebrew, which means to set aside. From what should they set aside the Sabbath? They were to set aside the Sabbath from secular days of the week, for the seventh day is different from the other six. For six days they should engage in secular works and business. However, on the Sabbath they should stop all works and businesses and spend the day only in relationship with God.

How could they set aside the Sabbath for God? The method was to *remember*. To remember the Sabbath does not mean simply to remember intelligently, but rather to regenerate the past. That is,

---

4. Ibid., 35.

the Israelites were to remember the two works of creation and redemption that God accomplished for their forefathers and they were to worship such a God. By doing so, they received a new energy from God.[5]

The Israelites had to remember the Sabbath and *observe it holy*. God commanded it repeatedly and with emphasis. *Take heed to all that I have said to you...* (Exodus 23:13). Of course, according to the previous verse, this commandment to keep the Sabbath is a solemn one (Exodus 23:12). Later in the same book we see a much stronger commandment: *Six days shall work be done, but on the seventh day you shall have a holy Sabbath of solemn rest to the Lord; whoever does any work on it shall be put to death* (Exodus 35:2).

In fact, a man did violate this commandment, which resulted in his relentless death. *While the Israelites were in the wilderness, they found a man gathering sticks on the Sabbath day... all the congregation brought him outside the camp, and stoned him to death with stones, as the Lord commanded Moses* (Numbers 15:32, 36). The Israelites had to keep the Sabbath in accordance with the solemn commandment of God, or die because of not doing so.

Accordingly, why did God command so solemn a commandment to the Israelites? He did so because of the special covenantal relationship between God and them. Moses explains it as follows:

> Six days shall work be done, but the seventh day is a Sabbath of solemn rest, holy to the Lord; whoever does any work on the Sabbath shall be put to death. Therefore the Israelites shall keep the Sabbath, observing the Sabbath throughout their generations, as a perpetual covenant. It is a sign forever between me and the Israelites....(Exodus 31:15-17).

Those who did not observe the Sabbath had to be killed. The reason is simple! The Sabbath is a sign of the everlasting covenant between God and the Israelites. In other words, by keeping the Sabbath one time per week, the Israelites demonstrated to the world that they were the people of a special covenant with God. Outwardly, they demonstrated this to the world, and inwardly, they enjoyed and relished the covenant relationship.

---

5. Ibid., 33-34.

When the Sabbath was enacted for the Israelites, no country had such a law. Only the Israelites enjoyed the Sabbath and the covenantal relationship with God. They became the special people who worshipped God, resting in His honor one time per week. This way of life inspired them to become more excellent people than people who did not worship God. As a result, the Sabbath also became an important element for the Israelites as they grew to become a distinctive nation different from other nations.[6]

A momentum existed that spurred the Sabbath to become a more important day for the Israelites. The Israelites had lost their country because of idolatry. Their country and the holy temple were entirely destroyed by Babylon. They could not worship God at the temple any more. Therefore, the Sabbath became a more important day for worship. Taking the Sabbath as the day to give to and worship God at the place where they stood, they enjoyed an incredible blessing that took the place of temple worship.[7]

Regulation of the Sabbath

The Sabbath is earnestly meant as a rest allowing for mental and spiritual recharging. For such a rest, the Israelites were clearly told the prohibited works. They could not bake on the Sabbath (Exodus 16:23). They could not plough or harvest (Exodus 34:21). They could not make fire anywhere (Exodus 35:3), nor gather sticks (Numbers 15:32 ff). They could not do business (Amos 8:5; Nehemiah 13:31), nor bear a heavy burden (Jeremiah 17:21-22).

Rabbis of Israel specifically illustrated the following thirty-nine regulations as prohibited works on the Sabbath:[8]

Sowing, plowing, reaps, binding sheaves;
Threshing, winnowing, selecting crops;
Grinding, sifting, kneading, baking;

---

6. A. Noordtzij, *Bible Student's Commentary: Leviticus*, Raymond Togtman, (Grand Rapids, MI: Zondervan Publishing House, 1982), 230.

7. That they lost their worship at the temple was not blessing, but curse. Nonetheless, having a system to be able to take the place of it was a blessing, not a curse. Yee, *Jewish Festivals and the Gospel of John*, 35.

8. See Mishnah Shabbat 7:2

Searing wool, washing it, beating it, dyeing it;
Spinning, weaving, making two loops, weaving two threads, separating two threads;
Tying, untying;
Sewing two stitches, tearing in order to sew two stitches;
Trapping a deer, slaughtering it, flaying it, salting it, curing its hide, scraping it, cutting it up;
Writing two letters, erasing two letters in order to write two letters;
Building, tearing down;
Putting out a fire, kindling a fire;
Hitting with a hammer
Transporting an object from one domain to another

The prohibited works were not only endlessly modified and expanded, but also strictly observed. A manuscript of the law found at an old synagogue near Cairo in 1896, had similar regulations to the aforementioned ones. Following are the regulations used in Damascus between first and third centuries:

> On the Sabbath day, no one is to speak of profane or vain matters. No one is to make loans to another. No one is to engage in litigation about property or profit. No one is to talk business.... No one is to go about in his field for the purpose of carrying on his normal work. On the Sabbath day, no one is to go out of the city beyond a distance of a thousand cubits. No one is to eat anything that has not been prepared beforehand.... When on a journey, no one is to partake of any food other than that which he previously had with him in his place of encampment.... No one is to draw water.... No one is to commission a non-Jew to do his own work. No one is to wear soiled garments or garments which have been worn while working in the garden except he wash them in water and scrub them with lye. No one is to observe a voluntary fast. No one is to follow his cattle to pasture beyond a distance of a thousand cubits.... No one is to bring anything into or out of his house.... Nurses are not to take their charges out on the Sabbath day. No one is to issue orders to his manservant or his maidservant or his hireling on the Sabbath day. No one is to assist an animal to give birth. If an animal fall into a pit or snare on the Sabbath day, no one is to lift it out; and if a human being fall into a well whence he

cannot be extricated by a ladder or a rope or any other instrument, no one is to lift him out....[9]

However, rabbis taught that one could transcend all regulations in some cases. Such cases were the following three: (1) cultic duties, (2) defensive warfare, and (3) the saving of life. First, in the case of circumcision, that is, if the eighth day when a baby should be circumcised after birth falls on the Sabbath, the circumcision could be practiced transcending the disciplines of the Sabbath day. Second, in the case of military warfare for the purpose of defending one's self and country, even if it is the Sabbath day, one could engage in the war. Third, in order to save life, Sabbath regulations could be suspended.[10]

Implementation of the Sabbath

Through the Sabbath, the Jewish people are enabled to have a fresh new week in which to spend their newly obtained energy. The Sabbath is implemented in the synagogue and the home. Starting with Friday night, after the Sabbath service at a synagogue, the father lays his hands on his children and pronounces the blessing.[11] To a son, he blesses, "May God make this son like Ephraim and Manasseh," and to a daughter, "May God make her like Sarah, Rebecca, Rachel and Leah."[12] Also, he chants to his wife, saying Proverbs 31:

> A good wife who can find?
> She is far more precious than jewels...
> She looks well to the ways of her household,
> and does not eat the bread of idleness.

---

9. Theodor H. Gaster, *A Modern Interpretation and Guide: Festivals of the Jewish Year* (H. Wolff, NY: William Sloane Associates Publishers, 1953), 269-270.

10. Yee, Jewish Festivals and the Gospel of John, 36-37.

11. According to Leviticus 23:32, the Sabbath is from the sunset on Friday (around 6 pm) to the sunset on Saturday (around 6 pm).

12. Gaster, *A Modern Interpretation and Guide: Festivals of the Jewish Year*, 279.

> Her children rise up and call her blessed;
> her husband also, and he praises her:
> Many women have done excellently,
> but you surpass them all.

On the next day, which is the Sabbath, they gather at the synagogue and study the Hebrew Bible and rabbinical literature, or listen to lectures from a rabbi or scholar. However, main events are practiced at home. Shortly before sunset on Friday, the mother spreads a clean white cloth on the table upon which she places two Sabbath loaves. Then, she lights the candles and pronounces the blessing: "Blessed are Thou, O Lord our God, King of the Universe, Who hast hallowed us by Thy commandments and commanded us to kindle the lamp."[13]

Worth noting is that the mother alone does not light the candles but does so with her oldest daughter. For them, to light the candles is a ceremony noting the beginning the Sabbath, but, at the same time, setting aside the Sabbath publicly (Exodus 20:8). Thanking God for giving them the Sabbath as an everlasting inheritance, they recite the Word of Genesis: *On the seventh day God finished his work which he had done, and he rested on the seventh day from all his work which he had done* (Genesis 2:2).

After lighting the candles, the mother gives thanks for the two loaves. The reason to prepare two loaves is in order to remember the fact that the Israelites gathered manna two times in the wilderness (Exodus 16:22, 29). The two loaves are covered with a small towel, which symbolizes the dew that covered the manna.[14] The Sabbath loaves were called **fine flour loaves** and offered as a fellowship offering to the Lord (Numbers 15:17-21).

At the conclusion of the Sabbath, that is, on Saturday evening, after finishing evening prayer, the father undertakes a ceremony. He prepares a special candle made of two intertwining pieces of wick, a box of spices, and a glass filled to overflowing with wine. He prays to the prophet Elijah that "the descendant of David" Messiah come speedily. He continues to thank God who distinguishes between sacred and profane, Israel and Gentile, and the Sabbath

---

13. Ibid., 275-6.
14. Ibid., 278.

and the weekdays. As he shares the glass of wine, he extinguishes the candle with spilled wine from the saucer.

Finally, the father recites Psalms 91:5-6: *You will not fear the terror of the night, nor the arrow that flies by day, nor the pestilence that stalks in darkness, nor the destruction that wastes at noonday*. Why is this Word recited during the Sabbath? The reason is simple! When they return to daily life and engage in secular business, they could be attacked by various temptations and tests. Therefore, the recitation serves as protection for them from all power of evil regardless of night or day. Also, the smell of the spices reminds them that they will be protected from the perils of the world.[15]

The Sabbath and Jesus

Jesus not only observed the Sabbath, but also newly interpreted its meaning, which is clear in the gospel of John. A sick man lived with a vain hope for thirty-eight years. In a sense, this man observed the Sabbath more strictly than anyone else because he had never walked the distance of 1000 cubits for the length of thirty-eight years. Not only on the Sabbath, but as if every day were the Sabbath, he had lain on one place without moving.[16]

Jesus healed this sick man on the Sabbath. By healing him, Jesus gave him a rest, although he compulsorily kept the regulations of the Sabbath. However, Jews swarmed like bees, refuting and persecuting Jesus, for they thought He clearly had violated the regulations of the Sabbath. They must have renounced Him because they thought He had transgressed the regulations of **tying** and **untying**. Their renouncement was due to Jesus' **work** of healing on the Sabbath (John 5:16).[17]

Jesus accounted for this, emphasizing **work**, as follows: *But Jesus answered them, My Father is* **working** *still, and I am* **working** (John 5:17). From this account, the most distinctive word is obvi-

---

15. Ibid., 275-7.
16. John Sungchul Hong, *Hyeondaineul Wihan BokeumJeondoui SeongKeyongjeok Model* (*Biblical Model of Evangelism for Modern People*), 2nd ed. (Seoul: Saebok Publish-ing House, 2010), 138.
17. See above, p. 29.

(John 5:17). From this account, the most distinctive word is obviously **work**. This must be a very clear paradox that work was emphasized on the Sabbath, underlining resting and worshipping. Later, Jesus re-mentioned this event saying that Jews were trying to kill Him because of the work of healing a disease: *Why do you seek to kill me? ... I did one deed, and you all marvel at it* (John 7:19, 21).

On the other Sabbath, Jesus healed a blind man. When His disciples asked why this man became blind, Jesus answered, again emphasizing **work**: *It was not that this man sinned, or his parents, but that the **works** of God might be made manifest in him. We must work the **works** of him ho sent me, while it is day; night comes, when no one can **work*** (John 9:3-4).

According to this saying, God **worked** again. After the first human being Adam disobeyed God, human beings suffered from many problems as the results of their sins and, among them, diseases existed. The man born blind needed a work of light. At last, God **worked** for him. Likewise, the impossibility existed that a man who had been ill for thirty-eight years as a result of the original sin could be healed without God's **work**.

The Lord of the Sabbath Jesus healed the blind man, who did not know a true rest for thirty-eight years, and gave him rest. By connecting diseases to sin, Jesus let him know that he could not have a rest physically or mentally because of sin: *See, you are well! Sin no more, that nothing worse befall you* (John 5:14). According to this saying, disease is a result of sin, and accordingly, Jesus showed that he also solved the problem of sin by healing the disease.[18]

Consequently, the teaching of *My Father is working still, and I am working* was a Word of notification that Jesus had come to the world for a purpose.[19] Jesus **worked** on the Sabbath in order to

---

18. Here sin is a cause of disease, but Jesus did not say that all diseases are a result of sin. Rather, he said not to sin in order to avoid "nothing worse" and it must mean eternal judgment, a result of sin. Andreas J. Kostenberger, *John: Baker Exegetical Commentary on the New Testament*, Robert Yarbrough & Robert H. Stein, ed. (Grand Rapids, MI: Baker Academic, 2004), 182.

give a true rest to those who kept the Sabbath but could not truly rest because of sin. The **work**, in a word, was recreation, that is, the **work** of redemption.[20] Otherwise, He would not have said the following: *For as the Father raises the dead and gives them life, so also the Son gives life to whom he will* (John 5:21).

In spite of so clear a work and Word, tied down to the regulations of the Sabbath, those who not only denied Jesus, the Lord of the Sabbath, but also eventually killed Him could not evade the responsibility. For this reason, immediately after He talked about the work of recreation, Jesus mentioned judgment (John 5:22); the judgment of those who rejected the Savior, who had healed the sick and blind men on the Sabbath, will receive. It is as Jesus said, *...you say, We see, your guilt remains* (John 9:41).

The Sabbath and the Lord's Day

The fourth commandment on the Sabbath, of the Ten Commandments, was very important for the Israelites; so much so that they kept the Sabbath once a week. They simply did not observe the Sabbath. They kept it in accordance with the various regulations. As mentioned earlier, its background was related to the creation of God. God created all things during six days and rested on the seventh day. So, the Israelites kept the Sabbath by recollecting the past.

However, Christians of the New Testament began to observe the Lord's Day instead of the Sabbath. They worshipped and shared bread together on the Lord's Day - *On the first day of the week, when we were gathered together to break bread...* (Acts 20:7). We can see the fact that they also rendered offerings as they worshipped - *On the first day of every week, each of you is to put something aside and store it up, as he may prosper, so that contributions need not be made when I come* (1 Corinthians 16:2).

---

19. In the text, the work of God and Jesus was to deliver human beings from sin and death and lead to eternal life. For this, see George R. Beasley-Murray, *John*, 2nd ed., Word Biblical Commentary, vol. 36, Ralph P. Martin, ed., (Nashville, TN: Thomas Nelson Publishers, 1999), 74.

20. Yee, *Jewish Festivals and the Gospel of John*, 44.

If so, why did Christians of the New Testament observe the Lord's Day instead of the Sabbath? The reason is also simple! Jesus Christ, who died on the cross for the redemption of human beings, was resurrected on the first day after the Sabbath. Because of the witness of resurrection, John had been once exiled to the Island of Patmos. As if He proved the witness of resurrection, Jesus Christ, the Lord of resurrection, appeared to John on "the Lord's Day," one the day of remembering His resurrection (Revelation 1:10).

As a result, unlike Jews of the Old Testament, Christians of the New Testament had the rest of recreation, not the rest of creation, by keeping the Lord's Day. The resurrection of the Lord provided many with liberation from guilt, which gave peace of mind. This peace will become the everlasting one when the Lord will come again. For this reason, Christians demonstrate a future-oriented and eschatological faith, expecting the Second Advent of the Lord and the fulfillment of recreation, by keeping the Lord's Day.[21]

---

21. Timothy C. Tennent, *Word Made Flesh!: Reflections on the Incarnation* (Wilmo-re, KY: Asbury Theological Seminary, 2009), 41.

Chapter 3

The Passover

The first festival presented in Leviticus 23 is Passover. Along with the Festival of Unleavened Bread and the Festival of First Fruits, Passover is one of the three festivals that comprise the festivals of spring. Prior to introducing Passover in the text, in verse 2, the already mentioned Word is repeated: *These are the appointed festivals of the Lord, the holy convocations, which you shall proclaim at the time appointed for them* (Leviticus 23:4). This repetition is due to the intention to earnestly introduce the other seven festivals.[1]

Historical Background

Leviticus 23:5 begins in the following way: *In the first month, on the fourteenth day of the month in the evening, is the Lord's passover.* This Passover originated with the liberation of the Israelites from Egypt. The Israelites came to live in Egypt because of their forefather Joseph. However, as time progressed, they became the slaves of Egypt, and thus endured unspeakable suffering (Exodus 1:12-14). At last they cried to God, and God listened to their prayers and intervened (Exodus 2:23-25).

God chose Moses as the leader and sent him to Pharaoh, the King of Egypt. The Word of God given to Pharaoh through Moses was to let the Israelites leave Egypt (Exodus 5:1). However, Pharaoh not only rejected the Word of God, but also denied even the existence of God (Exodus 5:2). Because of this negative response, God could not be quiet. If He had done so, then God would not have been realized as the Redeemer of Israel.

---

1. Roy Gane, *Leviticus, Numbers of the NIV Application Commentary* (Grand Rapi-ds, MI: Zondervan, 2004), 388.

God needed to show Pharaoh and the Egyptians the fact that He was able to save the Israelites. God warned Pharaoh and the Egyptians many times, often by administering disasters upon them. Pharaoh and the Egyptians always had the choice to acknowledge the existence and power of God. Although the disasters given to them were negative methods, the disasters were enough to display God's power (Exodus 9:14-6).

The miserable disasters of God started with blood and ended with blood. The first disaster was when God turned the water into blood. The last disaster occurred when all of the eldest sons and of the first born-animals were killed. God's ten disasters proceeded until their deaths, gradually and relentlessly. If Pharaoh and the Egyptians had accepted God earlier, they would not have been forced to see the deaths of their eldest sons. Their haughtiness and prejudice, however, drove them to a seemingly bottomless pit of death.

That night was a day when all of the eldest sons and animals were dying under God's judgment. During that dreary night, while the angels of death came to Egypt and gathered the lives of the elder sons and animals, an astounding event happened for the Israelites. Because the people were beloved by God as His elder (Exodus 4:22), although the eldest sons of Egypt were killed, the eldest sons of Israel were not killed. Instead, God let the eldest sons of Israel live by the killing of sacrificial lambs.

Enactment of Passover

These lambs that were killed instead of the eldest sons were the lambs of Passover. Although these lambs of Passover were killed in order to allow the eldest sons of Israel to live, their deaths became an obvious and serious warning concerning the death that would come to the Egyptians. The enactment of Passover is such a very important historical event that we need to study the process of the enactment.

> The Lord said to Moses and Aaron in Egypt, This month is to be for you the first month, the first month of your year. Tell the whole community of Israel that on the tenth day of this month each man is to take a lamb for his family, one for each household.

If any household is too small for a whole lamb, they must share one with their nearest neighbor, having taken into account the number of people there are. You are to determine the amount of lamb needed in accordance with what each person will eat. The animals you choose must be year-old males without defect, and you may take them from the sheep or the goats. Take care of them until the fourteenth day of the month, when all the people of the community of Israel must slaughter them at twilight. Then they are to take some of the blood and put it on the sides and tops of the doorframes of the houses where they eat the lambs. That same night they are to eat the meat roasted over the fire, along with bitter herbs, and bread made without yeast. Do not eat the meat raw or cooked in water, but roast it over the fire—head, legs and inner parts. Do not leave any of it till morning; if some is left till morning, you must burn it. This is how you are to eat it: with your cloak tucked into your belt, your sandals on your feet and your staff in your hand. Eat it in haste; it is the Lord's Passover. On that same night I will pass through Egypt and strike down every firstborn—both men and animals—and I will bring judgment on all the gods of Egypt. I am the Lord. The blood will be a sign for you on the houses where you are; and when I see the blood, I will pass over you. No destructive plague will touch you when I strike Egypt. "This is a day you are to commemorate; for the generations to come you shall celebrate it as a festival to the Lord—a lasting ordinance (Exodus 12:1-14).

From this passage, we learn the following important facts: first, the month that Passover was enacted should be the first month, January. As already mentioned in chapter two, both the sacred calendar and civil calendar existed. So, Passover was enacted in the first month of the sacred calendar. The reason God chose the first month is that the Israelites not only experienced the Exodus through Passover, but also were leaving to found a new and independent nation. Like the beginning of a new year, this was to be a fresh beginning for the Israelites.

Second, a lamb was needed for Passover. The lamb had to be qualified according to fastidious conditions. First, the lamb should be a one-year old male. The age of the lamb is important because this would indicate that the lamb had never copulated in order to produce its young. The lamb should be without blemish, otherwise it could not become the lamb of Passover.[2] Only the cleanest were acceptable as sacrifices to God.

Third, the lamb of Passover should be selected on the tenth day of the month and kept until the fourteenth day. On the fourteenth day, the Israelites had to kill the lamb and sprinkle some of its blood on the top and both sides of the doorframe of the houses. This was not to be done at their convenience. The instructions for the process were specifically clear (Exodus 12:22). They had to be followed precisely in order for the sacrifice of the lambs to work in the salvation of the eldest sons of Israel. If they did not follow God's rules precisely, none would be saved.

Fourth, those of the household who sprinkle the blood of the lamb on the door had to stay inside the house. God had to see the blood on the doorframe in order to know whose house to pass and they had to stay inside or they might die from the strength of God's passing. In the house, they were to eat the roasted lamb with unleavened bread and bitter herbs to remind them of their suffering as slaves in Egypt (Deuteronomy 16:3). They could not carry the flesh outside of their houses or break any of the bones (Exodus 12:46).

Fifth, if number of people in the household were too small to eat all of the lamb, they could invite another family to join them. This fact was an important revelation for the history of redemption. Until Passover a lamb had been killed for a man thus far. Now the scripture shows that a lamb was killed for a household. If the household was too small, they could invite their neighbors to join

---

2. The rule that animal should be without blemish is also seen in the rules of offerings: Animals blind or disabled or mutilated or having a discharge or an itch or scabs, you shall not offer to the LORD or make of them an offering by fire upon the altar to the Lord. A bull or a lamb which has a part too long or too short... Any animal which has its testicles bruised or crushed or torn or cut, you shall not offer to the Lord... (Leviticus 22:22-4). In fact, the Israelites had ever been scolded for offering with blemish. ...When you offer blind animals in sacrifice, is that no evil? And when you offer those that are lame or sick, is that no evil? (Malachi 1:8).

them. If a healthy lamb could be eaten by 10 people, it means that one lamb was sacrificed for ten people.³

Sixth, the Israelites had to take part in Passover, preparing for a journey. They had to eat in haste, with their cloaks and sandals on, while carrying their staffs. The time was full of expectancy; as if anything could happen. They had spent long 430 years in Egypt. Now they were to end the time of the suffering and leave their captors of centuries. Their journey was the end of the past and the beginning of the future. Their preparation for this journey was their active part in the festival called Passover.

The Practice of Passover

That night was one of tears. When God killed the eldest sons of Egypt and their animals, the Egyptians mourned bitterly (Exodus 12:30). In contrast, a different kind of cry must have arisen in the Israelites because the Egyptians, who had inflicted centuries of oppression and suffering, were judged; liberation from this lengthy oppression was imminent at last for the Israelites.

During that night, what made Egyptians and Israelites cry was death and life. Egyptians were killed because they rejected the Word of God, not killing sacrificial lambs. In contrast, however, the Israelites overcame death because they obeyed God by sacrificing lambs. The Israelites sprinkled lambs' blood on the doors and survived. The reason they survived is simple! When God passed over the houses smeared with blood, He saw that they had obeyed Him. Those in the blooded houses were not judged, but were instead passed over. Hence, Passover is the festival, in which God literally passed over those who had obeyed Him.⁴ The work of the Israelites was to believe in God and obey Him by smearing the

---

3. This revelation expanded as follows: while in the day of atonement a lamb or a goat was sacrificed for the Israelites, in the New Testament, a lamb Jesus died for theworld. For this, see the following article, John Sungchul Hong, "Weonhyeong Bokeum (Archetypical Gospel)," *Gyosu Nonchong*, v. 11 (2000): 746.

4. Passover is *phsah* (פֶּסַח) in Hebrew.

blood of a lamb on the door. The blood became a **sign** (Exodus 12:13).

The blood of the lamb became a sign of obedience to God. However, a study of Egyptian religion reveals an even deeper meaning of the sign. A male lamb is very important to the Egyptians because they served a god who looked like a male lamb, called *Amon*, who was regarded as a god of gods and as the foundation of all life on the earth and in the sky.[5] Therefore, Egyptians could not recklessly touch the animal, kill, or eat it. *Amon*'s power was believed to peak in January.[6] God's command to catch a male lamb, roast, and eat was for the Israelites an expression of obedience to God, but was a great challenge to the Egyptians. This was an effectively powerful tool used at Passover in the judgment on the god of Egypt (Exodus 12:12).

The redemption of Israel through Passover was the work of love on the side of God, but it was the work of liberation as seen by the Israelites. They could not easily forget this precious work, nor should they. For this reason, God commanded, *This day shall be for you a memorial day, and you shall keep it as a festival to the Lord; throughout your generations you shall observe it as an ordinance forever* (Exodus 12:14). In accordance with this commandment, the Israelites continued the festival of Passover (Joshua 5:10-11).

After the tabernacle was built, the Israelites observed Passover around it once a year, which was not difficult. After Solomon's temple was established, the distance to the temple was far away for some people, but did not seem to be a problem. They kept Passover by traveling to the temple to sacrifice a lamb. This annual practice continued until A.D. 70.

Replacement of the Passover Lamb

The Israelites saw many religious changes after A.D. 70. In that year, the army of Rome not only occupied Jerusalem, but also destroyed the temple to which the Israelites so gave importance. By

---

5. Kevin Williams, *The Holidays of God: Spring Festivals* (Grand Rapids, MI: RBC Ministries, 2000), 7.
6. Ibid., 7-8.

this, they lost the center for spiritual life. They could not worship in the temple or keep Passover because no temple existed for them to offer their sacrificial lambs.

So, did the Israelites neglect the commandment of God to keep Passover? God clearly commanded to keep this ordinance at its appointed time from year to year (Exodus 13:10). God also commanded they keep Passover in the place of God, that is, in the temple: You shall offer the passover sacrifice to the Lord your God, from the flock or the herd, at the place which the Lord will choose, to make his name dwell there (Deuteronomy 16:2). However, the place was destroyed.

Not only was the temple destroyed. Also, the priest, who caught a lamb and inaugurated the service of Passover with it, ceased to exist. The Israelites who lost the priest and the temple could only find a new method to keep God's commandment concerning Passover. The method was to prepare unleavened bread, that is, bread that does not include leaven (which causes bread to rise). Families began to observe Passover by eating unleavened bread.

Does the choice of replacing the sacrificial lamb with the eating of unleavened bread stand on legitimate ground? Yes, and the reason is based on an event that happened that night when the Israelites' forefathers left Egypt. The Israelites had to leave in haste because the Egyptians, who had lost their eldest sons, suddenly forced the Israelites to leave. Because of this urgency, they took their dough before it was leavened, their kneading bowls being bound up in their mantles on their shoulders and left Egypt (Exodus 12:34). Instead of the lamb of Passover, they ate unleavened bread brought out of Egypt on Passover.

Replaced Passover Service

Although the content and order of the Passover service changed as time progressed and according to places, the Israelites maintained the original framework in the following way. First, the father of a family sits at the front of a table, the youngest son on his right, and guests to his left side. The mother lights two candles and prays for blessing: "Blessed art thou, O Lord our God, King of the Universe,

Who has set us apart by His Word, and in whose Name we light the festival lights."[7]

In order to commemorate the promise of the fourfold redemption, four cups are prepared. God's promise in the Bible reads as follows: I will bring you out from under the burdens of the Egyptians; I will deliver you from their bondage; I will redeem you with an outstretched arm and with great acts of judgment; and I will take you for my people (Exodus 6:6-7). After father pours the wine into the first cup, which symbolizes the joy of the redemption, he lifts his cup toward heaven and prays to set aside the day. At this time, everyone rises from the table.

Next, they wash their hands. One of the family members takes a pitcher of water, bowl, and towel to all persons at the table so they can wash their hands. This allows for clean and proper handling of the food.

In the fourth step, they dip a green vegetable into the salt water and eat it. Green vegetables symbolize the season of spring, and the salt water symbolizes the tears of pain that were shed by the Israelites in slavery.

Fifth, after the father breaks in half the middle loaf of the prepared three unleavened breads, he put back the half, wraps the other half in a linen napkin, and hides it in the house. At this point the children close their eyes so they will not know the hidden place.

Sixth, in order to fulfill Exodus 12:26 that says the following: When your children say to you, What do you mean by this service?, he makes the youngest kid recite the following four questions:

1. On all other nights we eat either leavened or unleavened bread; why on this night do we eat only unleavened bread?
2. On all other nights we eat vegetables and herbs of all kinds; why on this night do we eat only bitter herbs?
3. On all other nights we do not think of dipping herbs in water or in anything else; why on this night do we dip

---

7. Howard & Rosenthal, *The Festival of the Lord*, 54. The explanation of the foll-owing services of Passover is based on this book.

the parsley in salt water and the bitter herbs in charoseth (It is like vinegar made of fruits and spices.)?
4. On all other nights we eat either sitting upright or reclining; why on this night do we eat reclining?[8]

Seventh, after father pours wine into the second cup, he explains the panoramic events that their ancestors experienced: the stories from Abraham to Isaac and Joseph, the story of their moving to Egypt, the exodus through Moses, the story of ten plagues, the story of the first Passover, the story of the giving of the Law, etc. Then Psalms 113-118 is recited. After this, the second cup is taken.[9]

Eighth, they wash hands again, break the upper unleavened bread and the remainder of the middle one into pieces, and distribute them to everyone. Each person eats bread dipped in the apple juice, which symbolizes the sweetness of God's redemption that they experienced in the middle of their bitter lives as slaves.

Ninth, they eat dinner. In the day of Jesus, they ate roasted lamb. However, the Jewish people of today also eat different foods such as fish, soup, chicken, carrots, fruit, and cake.

Tenth, they drink the third cup of wine, which is called "the cup of redemption." This is a name they use while waiting for the Messiah to be sent by God, who saved them from Egypt through the Passover. After the third cup, a child is sent to the front door to check on Elijah's arrival, so that when he comes, they receive him, drink wine with him, and he announces the Coming of the Messiah.

Eleventh, they drink the fourth cup of wine. At this point, they usually sing a hymn, read the latter half of the Hallel Psalms 115-118, and then conclude the worship with a conviction that God has joyfully accepted their Passover service.[10]

---

8. For the detailed explanation, see the book: William W. Francis, *Celebrate the Festivals of the Lord: The Christian Heritage of the Sacred Jewish Festivals* (Alexandria, VA: Crest Books, 1997), 21-2.

9. Psalms 113-118 is called the *Hallel*, which means "praise" in Hebrew. Howard & Rosenthal, *the Festivals of the Lord*, 57.

10. Epstein, *All about Jewish Holidays and Customs*, 62.

Passover and Sacrament

As mentioned earlier, unleavened bread was used instead of a Passover lamb, and service in the temple was replaced by service in the homes. Likewise, the Passover service in the New Testament was replaced by the sacrament. Jesus expanded Passover's meaning. On the night that Jews worshipped, remembering Passover, Jesus also inaugurated a service remembering Passover. He opened a new horizon for the festival of Passover.

Peter and John prepared a small supper by Jesus' instruction, which included bread (unleavened) and a cup of wine (Luke 22:8). Jesus did not regard unleavened bread and cup as simple dinner of the Passover. He applied them to Himself. He said, distributing a piece of bread to His disciples: *This is my body which is given for you. Do this in remembrance of me* (Luke 22:19).

After the disciples had eaten the bread, Jesus said, lifting the cup of wine: *This cup which is poured out for you is the new covenant in my blood* (Luke 22:20). According to this declaration of Jesus, unleavened bread and the cup of Passover were His body and blood. This enormous act of Jesus turned upside down the traditional service and its meaning. He gave a declaration to accept the Passover on a new dimension.

Passover was a service associated with the liberation of Israel. In other words, Passover was a festival only for Israel. For this reason, the Israelites strictly kept Passover in the homes even after the temple was destroyed. However, Jesus' Word of *this is my blood of the covenant, which is poured out for many for the forgiveness of sins* (Matthew 26:28), is a declaration that Passover exists for the Israelites as well as for all believers in Jesus Christ as the Messiah.

The comparison between the bread that Jesus distributed and the unleavened bread of Passover shows a close relationship between both. For the fifth order of the Passover service, three unleavened breads are prepared for and are hidden in a bag so that no one knows where they are. When the service is ripening, the leader takes the middle one out of the bag and breaks it into two pieces. He wraps one of the pieces in linen and hides it under pillow; the hidden piece is called *afikomen*.[11]

---

11. Williams, *The Holidays of God: Spring Festivals*, 10.

Children try to find the hidden *afikomen*, and whoever discovers it is rewarded. The father buys, opens, and distributes it to family members. The bread that Jesus distributed, saying, *Take, eat; this is my body*, must be this *afikomen*. Like the unleavened bread, Jesus was broken, wrapped in linen, and hidden. He was truly the bread of Passover for us.

In the service of Passover, the Jewish people prepared four cups. The first cup, as "the cup of sanctification," sanctified the supper of Passover. As "the cup of disaster," the second cup reminded them of disasters given to Egyptians. As "the cup of redemption," the third cup reminded them of the liberation of Israel. The fourth cup was "the cup of praise" used when singing Hallel as they concluded the service. Most notable of the four is of course, "the cup of redemption."

The cup that Jesus lifted, blessed, and distributed to his disciples was the very "cup of redemption." Just as the Jews shared the cup of wine after they ate *afikomen*, so Jesus took this cup after supper and said: *Drink of it, all of you; for this is my blood of the covenant, which is poured out for many for the forgiveness of sins* (Matthew 26:27-28). This cup was no longer only for the Israelites, but instead became the "the cup of redemption" for all sinners.

Chapter 4

Passover and Jesus

A lamb died for Passover. The lamb was a male lamb without blemish and one year old. The lamb died on behalf of the eldest sons of Israel. The family members, who evaded death by the death of the lamb, roasted it. They put the dried branch of a pomegranate tree in the mouth of the lamb throughout the entire animal.[1] After hanging the branch over the fire, they roasted the lamb, spinning it. Without breaking a born at all, they roasted it whole and ate it.

Lamb

Amazingly, John the Baptist in the New Testament called Jesus Christ a lamb. This name was not appropriate from the human perspective. How can a human being and even the Savior of the world Jesus Christ, become a lamb? One day of busily preparing for the way of the Messiah, John the Baptist declared: *Behold, the Lamb of God, who takes away the sin of the world!* (John 1:29).

What does this declaration of John the Baptist mean? Literally, it is a declaration that Jesus Christ is the very lamb of Passover. The declaration holds within it that the lamb of Passover should be without blemish; Jesus Christ has no blemish at all. If He had a small blemish, no matter how small it was, Jesus Christ could not have become the lamb of Passover.

---

1. Benno Jacob, *The Second Book of the Bible: Exodus*, Walter Jacob trans. (Hob-oken NJ: KTAV Publishing House, Inc., 1992), 306.

As if He supported this fact, Jesus Christ was born of a virgin. Like others, if He had been born by a union between husband and wife, He would have been an ordinary person and a sinner like others. However, Jesus Christ, who was born from a virgin by the work of the Holy Spirit, had no blemish or sin; In this, He was unlike others. Even Pilate who judged Him, declared to have found no crime in him (Matthew 26:23; John 19:4). Unblemished he lived a righteous life, a life for others and became the lamb of the Passover.

Listen to the words of a robber who was crucified along with Jesus: ...*this man has done nothing wrong* (Luke 23:41). Although He endured all kinds of trials and suffering, Jesus was without blemish. As if describing this aspect, the author of Hebrews describes Him as follows: ...*one who in every respect has been tempted as we are, yet without sin* (Hebrews 4:15).

The paschal lamb means a lamb to be killed. Jesus Christ, the paschal lamb rose again on the third day after his death. The fact that Jesus rose again was another important evidence, proving once more that He was without blemish and spot (Romans 1:4). If He had died for His own sin, He could not have been resurrected. However, His resurrection is enough to prove the fact that He died for others' sins, not for His own, for He had none (Romans 4:25).

The declaration of the author of Hebrews who astoundingly described Jesus Christ, who rose again, as high priest, is as follows: *For it was fitting that we should have such a high priest, holy, blameless, unstained, separated from sinners, exalted above the heavens* (Hebrews 7:26). Jesus Christ is the high priest who can lead us sinners to God because He is sinless and unstained.

Why did John the Baptist call Jesus Christ a lamb? Jesus was a healthy young man in his thirties (Luke 3:23). The lamb of Passover was one year old and so this lamb was called a young lamb. The question of a male lamb is easily solved. Since Jesus was a man, He was described as a male lamb. However, what is the relationship between one year old lamb and Jesus Christ of thirties?

As mentioned above, the Israelites who raised lambs wanted to produce lambs and raise them well. In order to do so, the first important act was to produce the healthy young stock. For this, they restricted male lambs from mating for one whole year because they believed that only a male lamb one year old could produce the healthy young stock. As a result, one year old male lamb designates wholly mature but not mated yet.

Now we can understand why Jesus Christ was called a lamb without blemish. Jesus was a wholly mature and healthy man. He was a qualified person who had everything. However, He did not go the way of a man like other men. He was unmarried. He did not live a life to produce a family and search for happiness. Instead, He offered His body as an offering for others (Hebrews 9:12).

For this sublime purpose, Jesus played the role of a lamb. Just as the lamb of Passover died for the eldest sons of Israel, so Jesus Christ died on the cross for sins of all human beings. John the Baptist, who understood this aspect, proclaimed: *Behold, the Lamb of God, who takes away the sin of the world* (John 1:29). "The sin of the world" here is more expanded than the original concept of the lamb of Passover.

The lamb, who takes away the sin of the world, combines two concepts of the Old Testament; the lamb of Passover and the lamb who is led to a slaughter. The latter designates the servant of suffering, who bore our sins (Isaiah 53:6-7). The servant of suffering was also called a lamb (Isaiah 53:7) and bore the following work: *He was wounded for our transgressions, he was bruised for our iniquities* (Isaiah 53:5).

John the Baptist who called Jesus Christ *the Lamb of God, who takes away the sin of the world*, supplied the content that combined the two concepts. Like the lamb of Passover that suffered and died so that others would live, the lamb of God without any blemish willingly suffered but not only for the elder sons of the families of Israel, but for all the sinners.[2] Yes, it was Jesus Christ who as the lamb of Passover willingly accepted death for the sake of others.

Jesus had to die the Paschal lamb on the Passover. The Bible clearly mentions the fact in John 18:28: *Then they led Jesus from the house of Caiaphas to the praetorium. It was early. They themselves did not enter the praetorium, so that they might not be defiled, but might eat the Passover.* Like the lamb of Passover, Jesus'

---

2. Yee, *Jewish Festivals and the Gospel of John*, 60.

bones were not broken at all (Exodus 12:46; John 19:36).[3] In fact, Jesus was the true ultimate sacrificial lamb of Passover.

Time of Death

During that night when the Israelites came out of Egypt, they killed lambs and smeared their blood on the doors. God clearly informed them of the date and time to kill the lambs. The first was the month: *This month shall be for you the beginning of months; it shall be the first month of the year for you* (Exodus 12:2). The second was the day: *On the tenth day of this month they shall take every man a lamb* (Exodus 12:3). The third was the time: *You shall keep it until the fourteenth day of this month, when the whole assembly of the congregation of Israel shall kill their lambs in the evening* (Exodus 12:6).

Amazingly, the date and time of the lambs' deaths correspond to the date and time that the Paschal lamb Jesus died. The date that Jesus finally went to Jerusalem was the tenth day of Nissan. According to the gospel of John, Jesus arrived in Bethany on the sixth day before Passover (John 12:1). Jesus left on the ninth day and entered Jerusalem on the next, or tenth day, (John 12:12).

Of course, Jesus entered Jerusalem on the tenth day in order to be killed as the lamb of Passover. Without error of one day, this is exactly the same date that the Israelites took the lambs on the tenth day of January.[4] On that day, Jesus sat on a donkey and entered Jerusalem as the Messiah who was prophesized about in the Old

---

3. When a person is crucified, his body sags so that it cannot breathe. This causes him to push himself up with his heels just long enough to take a deep breath. Therefore, if his legs are broken, he would not be able to breathe so he would die earlier. The Jewish people tried to break Jesus' heel. However, since He had already died, they did not have to do that. As a result, as the Bible said, not one of His bones was broken. Richard Booker, *Celebrating Jesus in the Biblical Festivals* (Shippenburg, PA Destiny Image Publishers, Inc., 2009), 43-34.

4. According to Daniel B. Wallace, the professor of the New Testament at Dallas Theological Seminary, the year that Jesus died was 33 AD, and January 10 of the year was Monday. http://bible.org/article/passover-time-Jesus: "Passover in the Time of Jesus" by Daniel B. Wallace.

Testament (Zechariah 9:9). Many people welcomed Him and accepted. He was the Messiah. However, Jesus was not the type of Messiah that they had anticipated.

Interestingly, the lamb of Passover was taken on the tenth day and killed on the fourteenth day. Why did they let the lamb wait five days for death? The reason is also clear. They wanted to meticulously check that the lamb was without blemish, male, and one year old. This lamb was one that would die for the eldest sons of Israel. In order to be offered to God, the lamb should be perfect.

That being the case, why did the Paschal lamb Jesus Christ enter Jerusalem five days before Passover? The reason is also obvious! He also needed to be meticulously investigated during the period. He was a sacrificial offering who would be offered to God for the sins and judgment of all human beings. The lamb that would do such an invaluable task had to be without any blemish.

The leaders of Judaism asked for the task of scrupulously investigating and testing Jesus. None were as excellent as they were in catching flaws and administering tests based on the law. The Pharisees and the Sadducees made a frantic attempt to catch flaws in Jesus by asking Him difficult questions. However, no person or question produced flaws in Him (Matthew 22:34, 46).

When their methods were completely used up, the leaders of Judaism sent Jesus to Pilate as the last resort. The governor Pilate was good at dealing with sinners. By dealing with Jesus using the carrot-and-stick method, Pilate did his best at catching Jesus' flaws. However, Pilate concluded: *See, I am bringing him out to you, that you may know that I find no crime in him* (John 19:4).

The lamb of Passover was killed at sunset on January 14, which means 3 P.M. Since a new day begins after 3 P.M., the day was Friday. Jesus was also captured during the night that Friday began and was crucified at 9 A.M. in the morning: *It was the third hour, when they crucified him* (Mark 15:25). Of course, the third hour here means 9 A.M. So, what happened before Jesus was crucified?

Jesus inaugurated the last sacrament for His disciples from 6 to 9 in the evening. Then He went to Gethsemane and prayed the famous prayer of agony. Since His agony was intensely deep, His sweat formed like drops of blood, falling down from His face

(Luke 22:44). Around midnight, the subordinates that the religious leaders and the army leaders sent, arrested Jesus (John 18:12).

Jesus was dragged between places all night. Jesus was first interrogated by Caiaphas, the high priest of the year, and by Caiaphas' father-in-law Annas (Matthew 26:57; John 18:13). He was grilled first by Pilate who then sent him to Herod (Mark 15:1; Luke 23:6 ff), who then sent Him back to Pilate for final interrogation. Pilate then sentenced Jesus to death as the religious leaders of Israel and the general public wanted (Luke 23:24).

Like this, Jesus, who not only was interrogated all night long, but also was harshly whipped, walked to Mount Calvary, with a cross laid on his back (Luke 23:26). As mentioned above, He was crucified at 9 A.M., Friday, on the cross he had carried. The sixth hour, that is, at noon, the sky and the earth went in the dark, and all stayed dark until 3 P.M., when Jesus died (Mark 15:33-34, 37).

As mentioned above, the Sabbath is from the evening of Friday to the evening of Saturday. The Bible clearly mentions that Jesus died on the cross, comparing it to the day of preparation, or, the day before Passover: *Since it was the day of Preparation, in order to prevent the bodies from remaining on the cross on the Sabbath (for that Sabbath was a high day), the Jews asked Pilate that their legs might be broken, and that they might be taken away* (John 19:31).

The expression that "Sabbath is a high day" draws its meaning from these festivals. The Jewish people kept the Festival of Unleavened Bread for seven days after Passover and among the seven days, the first and the last days, were considered as special days, or days to have to do no work (Leviticus 23:7-8). The Bible called these two days **high days**, and in the week that Jesus died, the Sabbath and the high day overlapped. On the very special day of a holy assembly, Jews could not hang the dead body of Jesus on the cross.

The month that the lamb of Passover was killed became the first month of the year, the month that God liberated Israel from Egypt for them to start a new independent nation. Since Jesus died as the lamb of Passover, who was liberated? And, did a new independent nation start? Of course, yes. Jesus' death became the starting point of a much greater history than the liberation and the independence of Israel.

The death of Jesus Christ was a great work allowing many people to receive a salvation that transcends ethnicity and race (Revelation 7:9-10). Countless people were liberated from sin before the cross. The liberated people formed a church and began to accomplish the Kingdom of God that does not belong to the world (Revelation 1:5-6). This magnificent work surpasses the work of the Exodus thousands of times. This was a splendid work that the Paschal lamb Jesus Christ accomplished.

Place of Death

The Israelites killed lambs of Passover for the Exodus, sprinkled their blood on the doors, and ate the flesh in their homes. However, to take the lamb of Passover in this way was just one time in history. As the result of the Passover, the Israelites were liberated from Egypt and began to proceed to Canaan for the formation of an independent nation. Nevertheless, God commanded them to keep the Passover forever.

The place that the lamb of Passover died could not be changed. For this reason, God naturally and additionally explained about the place to the Israelites who had left Egypt. For the explanation, let us see Deuteronomy: You may not offer the Passover sacrifice within any of your towns which the Lord your God gives you; but at the place which the Lord your God will choose, to make his name dwell in it...(Deuteronomy 16:5-6). Place is the emphasis here. The Israelites had to offer the sacrifice of Passover only at the place God directly chose. Where was this place? The place was where Jesus Christ would die; Golgatha, a place all Christians know well.

Why did God choose Golgotha? In order to understand, let us study the work of David. David was deceived by the strategy of Satan; he commanded a count of the number of the Israelites, that is, a census. God had always let Israel know the law of a census. According to the law, all over twenty had to give a half of a shekel as redemption money (Exodus 30:11-16).

However, David seems to have had enough pride to neglect God's law. He was originally a humble person, but became an arrogant person at the time. As a result, God sent pestilence to David and his country, and thus 70,000 died. Returning to his original humility, he deeply repented, which God accepted (1 Chronicles 21:16-17).

Although God accepted David's repentance, David had to be forgiven in accordance with the law. God gave him the Word of grace to build an altar to the Lord on the threshing floor of Ornan and offer the sin offering (1 Chronicles 21:18). When David did as God commanded, God responded and forgave him. Interestingly, who could know that the threshing floor of Ornan that God chose would become the place where the Paschal lamb Jesus would die?

When David's son Solomon built a temple, he chose the place where the threshing floor of Ornan was, which became the very Mount Moriah. The Bible explains this information thus: Then Solomon began to build the house of the Lord in Jerusalem on Mount Moriah, where the Lord had appeared to David his father, at the place that David had appointed, on the threshing floor of Ornan the Jebusite (2 Chronicles 3:1).

When He told the Israelites who experienced the Exodus to offer Passover at the place that the Lord your God will choose, to make his name dwell in it (Deuteronomy 16:6), God had already mentioned the place. It can be found in the commandment given the forefather of Israel Abraham. God commanded Abraham to offer his son Isaac as a burnt offering, and its place was the very Mount Moriah.

Let us review the Word that God gave Abraham: Take your son, your only son Isaac, whom you love, and go to the land of Moriah, and offer him there as a burnt offering upon one of the mountains of which I shall tell you (Genesis 22:2). They offered a burnt offering at a place in the land of Moriah about which God had told them (Genesis 22:9). Of course, the offering was a male lamb, not Isaac. From that time on, the place was called the mountain of the Lord (Genesis 22:14).[5]

---

5. According to Jubilees, a book prior to Christianity, the date that Abraham offered Isaac as an offering was the fourteenth day of Nissan, and it was a typology of the lamb of Passover. Michael Green, *Evangelism in the Early Church*, 4th ed. (Grand Rapids, MI: William B. Eerdmans Publishing Co, 1977), 111.

Keep in mind, Mount Moriah was where God met Abraham in the special way. God chose the same place to offer the service of Passover, and chose the same Mount for David's atonement of sin, and right on the same spot our Paschal Lamb Jesus Christ died on the cross as the ultimate Passover lamb. Jesus Christ was brought to Golgotha, the place of the skull, where He was crucified (Matthew 27:22).

What does Golgotha have to do with Mt. Moriah? Simply put, Golgotha is the summit of Mt. Moriah, and therefore both Golgotha and Mt. Moriah are identical. Of course, Mt. Moriah is much larger than its summit. When God designated Mt. Moriah to Abraham and David, He had Golgotha in mind as well.[6]

As if to prove He is the Paschal lamb, Jesus Christ appeared in the temple on the Passover. Driving sheep and cattle with a whip, He said the following: *You shall not make my Father's house a house of trade* (John 2:16). The angered Jews asked him for a sign, but Jesus answered strangely: *Destroy this temple, and in three days I will raise it up* (John 2:19).

Directly speaking, the meaning of this weird saying is as follows: "It means that Jesus died on the cross to forgive all sinners who are threatened the judgment of sin, being absorbed by guilt like David. It also means that although he died so, Jesus lived again after three days, as when Abraham offered Isaac as a burnt offering, he had Isaac back."[7]

The Paschal lamb Jesus Christ was also sacrificed on Mount Moriah. The reason that He followed the footsteps of Abraham and David is that Moriah was the place God had fixed. Jesus Christ died on Mount Moriah, not in the temple made by human beings. Like a burnt offering of Abraham and a sin offering of David, Jesus Christ died on the cross that was erected at Golgotha on Mount Moriah. At Golgotha, His body got torn, and His blood was shed at the place of God's choosing.

---

6. See http://www.ensignmessage.com/archives/moriah.html

7. John Sungchul Hong, *Hananimui Saramdeul: Mataebogeum iljang iljeol Ganghaeseolgyo* (*The People of God: Sermons on Matthew 1:1*), (Seoul: Saebok Publishing House, 2005), 32-33.

Meaning of Death

After they smeared the blood of the lambs of Passover on the doors, the Israelites ate the flesh in the houses in the following way:

> They shall eat the flesh that night, roasted; with unleavened bread and bitter herbs they shall eat it. Do not eat any of it raw or boiled with water, but roasted, its head with its legs and its inner parts... you shall not break a bone of it (Exodus 12:8-9, 46).

In other words, the lamb of Passover shed its blood for the redemption of the Israelites, and its body was ripped apart to become food.

Designating His body on the Passover as if He were this lamb of Passover, Jesus Christ said:[8]

> Unless you eat the flesh of the Son of man and drink his blood, you have no life in you; he who eats my flesh and drinks my blood has eternal life, and I will raise him up at the last day. For my flesh is food indeed, and my blood is drink indeed (John 6:53-55).

Through its blood and food, the lamb of Passover saved the Israelites from death and opened the way of liberation. However, the Paschal lamb Jesus Christ died not only for the Israelites' liberation, but also to liberate the world from its sins and judgment. To emphasize this fact, Jesus said: *He who eats my flesh and drinks my blood has eternal life, and I will raise him up at the last day* (John 6:54).

The Israelites believed in God, killed a lamb, stroked the blood on the door, roasted and ate the lamb just as God told them to do. If they had not believed in the Word of God, they might not have escaped the imminent judgment. Likewise, Jesus promised that those who did as He said to *eat my flesh* and *drink my blood* have *eternal life* and *will raise up at the last day.*

Jesus had already explained this act of eating and drinking in detail: ... *he who believes has eternal life* (John 6:47). As a result, this act means faith. Jesus Christ's body was torn and shed blood

---

8. There are scholars who argue that the body and the blood of Jesus must be the background of the blood and the flesh of the Passover lamb. Craig S. Keener, *The Gospel of John: A Commentary*, vol. 1 (Peabody, MA: Hendrickson Publishers, Inc., 2003), 688.

on the cross for sinners. If sinners believe and accept the fact that Jesus Christ was torn and shed blood for them, they will have eternal life as He promised.[9]

From this perspective, the proclamation of John the Baptist will open a new horizon: *Behold, the Lamb of God, who takes away the sin of the world* (John 1:29). In particular, the meaning of the expression of "**the sin of the world**" bears important. Here we should notice that **sin** is in singular, not the plural. **Sin** in plural indicates the actions of sin to commit specifically; in the singular the word means the whole of sin that interrupts connection between God and people,[10] thus causing them to be in sin. In other words, the word sin includes sin to transgression of God's law, which ranges from distrust to disruption coming before Jesus Christ.[11]

The gospel of John describes Jesus Christ as the Paschal lamb in three aspects, which upset the customs and thoughts that the Israelites had traditionally kept. The first aspect was the teaching that the Paschal lamb Jesus Christ took the place of the temple (John 2:19). The second as the proclamation that the lamb of Passover Jesus Christ took the place of Moses and manna (John 6:32-33). The third was the fact that the Paschal lamb Jesus Christ replaced all of the lambs offered in the temple to that point (John 19:31-36).[12]

The fact that the Paschal lamb Jesus Christ was sacrificed urges all Christians to live holy lives. Paul associated the sacrifice of Jesus with the holiness of Christians as follows: *Cleanse out the old leaven that you may be a new lump, as you really are unleavened. For Christ, our paschal lamb, has been sacrificed. Let us celebrate... with the unleavened bread of sincerity and truth* (1 Corinthians 5:7-8).

As a result, the death of the Paschal lamb Jesus Christ teaches Christians the following three things: first, we are saved when we

---

9. Arthur W. Pink, *Exposition of the Gospel of John* (Grand Rapids, MI: Zondervan Publishing House, 1968), 347.

10. Martha Zimmerman, *Celebrating Biblical Festivals* (Minneapolis, MN: Bethany House, 2004), 54.

11. Keener, *The Gospel of John*, 456.

12. Yee, *Jewish Festivals and the Gospel of John*, 60.

accept the Lamb with belief, which is also the starting point of the life of faith; second, Christians should live holy lives based on the sacrifice of the Lamb; and third, on the last day, Christians will have eternal life with Christ and reign on earth (Revelation 5:9).

Chapter 5

Unleavened Bread

The second festival presented in Leviticus 23 is the Festival of Unleavened Bread.[1] It is also called the festival of bread made without leaven (Exodus 23:15), which means the festival to eat bread that does not include leaven. As mentioned above, the Festival of Unleavened Bread formulates the three festivals of spring, along with Passover and the Festival of First Fruits. Located between Passover and the Festival of First Fruits, this festival conveys an important meaning. This festival lasts for seven days, of which the first and last days are the Sabbath.

Biblical Background

In order to study the biblical background of this festival, let us return to the Bible. Leviticus describes the Festival of Unleavened Bread as follows:

> On the fifteenth day of that month the Lord's **Festival of Unleavened Bread** begins; for seven days you must eat bread made without yeast. On the first day hold a sacred assembly and do no regular work. For seven days present an offering made to the Lord by fire. And on the seventh day hold a sacred assembly and do no regular work (Leviticus 23:6-8).

---

1. The Festival of Unleavened Bread is called *hag ha matzot* (גח תצמה) in Hebrew.

The Festival of Unleavened Bread starts on the fifteenth day of Nissan. The date is the next day of Passover, which continues for seven days and ends on the twenty-first day. Since Passover and the Festival of Unleavened Bread coincide on this day, they are also called Passover for eight days and the Festival of Unleavened Bread for eight days.[2] Why should the Israelites eat bread that does not include yeast on this festival? In order to answer this question, let us read euteronomy:

> You shall eat no leavened bread with it; seven days you shall eat it with unleavened bread, the bread of affliction—for you came out of the land of Egypt in hurried flight—that all the days of your life you may remember the day when you came out of the land of Egypt (Deuteronomy 16:3).

From this passage, we learn the two reasons. First, since the Israelites urgently escaped from Egypt at night, they had no time to make bread made with yeast. The second reason was for the sake of remembering the day.

For the Israelites, the day was such an important day they could not help but remember. It was the day that three million young and old people moved as a great army and with all of their livestock, and experienced the Exodus. It was the day that changed them from the status of slaves to that of free people. Moses described the experience in this way: *They set out from Rameses in the first month, on the fifteenth day of the first month; on the day after the Passover the Israelites went out triumphantly in the sight of all the Egyptians* (Numbers 33:3). In order to remember the day of miracle for them to have escaped from Egypt, the place of suffering, the Israelites ate bread made without yeast.

While both Passover and the Festival of Unleavened Bread were enacted before the Exodus, the remaining five festivals were enacted after the Exodus. Those two festivals were important festivals for the Israelites to the extent that they were directly related to the Exodus. In other words, the festivals were important ones to commemorate the historical event of leaving Egypt where the Israelites

---

2. Howard & Rosenthal, *The Festival of the Lord*, 65.

had endured all kinds of sufferings for four hundred thirty years to then enter a new life.

According to the Word of God, God's instructions associated with the Festival of Unleavened Bread were only three. The first was an offering every day by fire for seven days of the Festival of Unleavened Bread, at the place which God chose *to make his name dwell in it*, that is, in the temple (Deuteronomy 16:2). Instructions in Leviticus 23 read as follows: *You shall present an offering by fire to the Lord seven days.* Of course, an offering by fire means offering a sacrifice to God by burning it with fire.

What did the Israelites have to offer by fire? Could they select the offering themselves? Of course, not! They could never select offerings at their convenience. They had to offer an offering that God appointed. In order to prevent the occurrence of an offering of convenience, God instructed a kind and a number of offering in detail, which is included in Numbers:

> Present to the Lord an offering made by fire, a burnt offering of two young bulls, one ram and seven male lambs a year old, all without defect. With each bull prepare a grain offering of three-tenths of an ephah of fine flour mixed with oil; with the ram, two-tenths; and with each of the seven lambs, one-tenth. Include one male goat as a sin offering to make atonement for you. Prepare these in addition to the regular morning burnt offering. In this way prepare the food for the offering made by fire every day for seven days as an aroma pleasing to the Lord; it is to be prepared in addition to the regular burnt offering and its drink offering (Numbers 28:19-24).

The Israelites had to offer a lamb in the morning and evening every day. Whenever they offered a lamb, they had to offer fermented liquor as the drink offering at the same time (Numbers 28:3-8). God said they should not omit the burnt offering in the morning and evening, when they presented an offering by fire at the Festival of Unleavened Bread. So, during the seven days, they had to present an offering by fire at the Festival of Unleavened Bread, in addition to the burnt offering presented in the morning and evening.

A kind and number of animals for an offering by fire at the Festival of Unleavened Bread are surprisingly numerous. They are two young bulls, one ram, seven male lambs a year old, and one male goat. Therefore, they should offer eleven animals of four kinds by an offering by fire every day. When they presented these offerings, they were to add a cereal offering of fine flour.[3] The quantity of barley flour was also a great deal. Since a tenth of an ephah corresponds to two liters, they offered thirty liters of flour in total, as an offering by fire every day.

The second instruction of God related to the Festival of Unleavened Bread was that they could not do any work on the first and the last days of the Festival of Unleavened Bread. The Israelites had to gather as a holy assembly instead of an assembly concerning business (Exodus 12:16; Leviticus 23:7-8; Numbers 28:25; Deuteronomy 16:8). Of course, presenting various offerings, they worshipped God who received the offerings. However, resting for two of the seven days, they thanked God who gave all blessings—the Almighty God who had delivered them from Egypt and the God of love who had allowed them to harvest the barley.[4]

The third instruction of God related to the Festival of Unleavened Bread was to strictly prohibit leaven. During this period, they could not eat bread made with yeast, and it should not even exist around them, no matter how small. God mentioned this clearly and emphatically so that no one could misunderstand this prohibition. He also repeatedly instructed it. God prohibited leaven at six places, at least, in the Pentateuch (Exodus 14:14-20; 13:6-8; 23:15; 34:18; Leviticus 23:6; Deuteronomy 16:3, 8). Additionally, God clearly stated the punishment of the violation of this prohibition so that they would not misunderstand.

> For seven days you are to eat bread made without yeast. On the first day remove the yeast from your houses, for whoever eats anything with yeast in it from the first day through the seventh must be cut off from Israel… In the first month you are to eat bread made without yeast, from the evening of the fourteenth day until the evening of the twenty-first day. For seven days no yeast is to

---

3. Since the Festival of Unleavened Bread was the harvest of barley, they made
flour of barley as the cereal offering. Noordtzij, *Bible Student's Commentary: Leviticus*, 23
4. Ibid.

be found in your houses. And whoever eats anything with yeast in it must be cut off from the community of Israel, whether he is an alien or native-born. Eat nothing made with yeast. Wherever you live, you must eat unleavened bread (Exodus 12:15, 18-20).

According to this passage, leaven was to be removed **from houses** of the Israelites. God gradually expanded the realm that leaven should be removed: ... *no leaven shall be seen with you in all your territory* (Exodus 13:7). **"Your territory"** means the place where an individual person of Israel dwells. The next step was wider territory: *No leaven shall be seen with you in all your territory for seven days* (Deuteronomy 16:4). **"In all your territory"** here means the entire country. In a word, during the Festival of Unleavened Bread, leaven was not to be seen anywhere in Israel.

Cultural Application

As mentioned in the chapter on Passover, in A.D. 70, an event occurred that thoroughly changed their way of life. The temple was destroyed, and the position of the priest disappeared. Accordingly, all services in the temple were also abolished. The Israelites were unable to keep the following commandment any more: *At the place which the Lord your God will choose... For six days you shall eat unleavened bread; and on the seventh day there shall be a solemn assembly to the Lord your God; you shall do no work on it* (Deuteronomy 16:7-8).

Just as the Israelites kept Passover by eating unleavened bread instead of the lamb of Passover at each home, so they kept the Festival of Unleavened Bread at each home. The preparation for the Festival of Unleavened Bread is the job of mothers. In order to remove all leavens, mothers give the house a good spring-cleaning. Since all leavens should be removed, they sweep, ransack, and wipe. They find leaven, mop, wash dishes with hot water, and empty cupboards of any leaven.[5]

---

5. Williams, *The Holidays of God: Spring Festivals*, 16.

On the eve of Passover, a family gathers together and inaugurates the celebration of "finding leaven." To begin, they recite the following three verses from Exodus 12:[6]

> Seven days you shall eat unleavened bread; on the first day you shall put away leaven out of your houses, for if any one eats what is leavened, from the first day until the seventh day, that person shall be cut off from Israel (Exodus 12:15); For seven days no leaven shall be found in your houses; for if any one eats what is leavened, that person shall be cut off from the congregation of Israel, whether he is a sojourner or a native of the land (Exodus 12:19); It was a night of watching by the Lord, to bring them out of the land of Egypt; so this same night is a night of watching kept to the Lord by all the Israelites throughout their generations (Exodus 12:42).

After this, the father holds an old wooden spoon in one hand and a goose feather in the other. After turning off the light, by candlelight he searches from room to room in order to find any leaven. Following him, the children see that he carefully sweeps bread that he finds onto the wooden spoon. They also see that he wraps the pieces of leaven, the wooden spoon, and the feather in a paper bag and ties it with a thread.[7]

If the mother thoroughly cleaned the house, no leaven would be found. However, for the celebration of "finding leaven," mother cuts white bread made with leaven into twelve pieces and leaves them in rooms, and on a window frame. If the father, along with his children, finds the pieces by candlelight, he puts them in a paper bag, along with the feather and the wooden spoon. After praying together, they read Psalms 103:12: *As far as the east is from the west, so far does he remove our transgressions from us.*[8]

---

6. Zimmerman, *Celebrating Biblical Festivals*, 58.

7. Howard & Rosenthal, *The Festivals of the Lord*, 67.

8. Some scholars explain comparing the Jewish practice that finds yeast with the Christian faith: 1.You cannot go off alone—you need the light of Christ to find your way. 2. The light (Christ) exposes the bread (sin). 3. Mother may forget where she put some of the pieces—some sins in our lives are forgotten until the light of Christ shed light on them. 4. Some pieces are hard to find—some of our sins are hidden too deeply. Zimmerman, *Celebrating Biblical Festivals*, 58-60,

The father and the children go with the bag outside the house. At this point, the fathers and children of other families gather together at one place with their bags. After building a fire, they put their bags in the fire one by one. The more bags added, the higher the fire. As night deepens, the flame wanes, and people gradually go back home. What is left are only gray ashes and the smoldering bread pieces.[9]

Then, the Israelites are ready to have Passover and the Festival of Unleavened Bread. The reason is clear! As time passes, leaven came to symbolize the life of oppression they had lived as slaves in Egypt. Of course, such a life was opposed to God's will because it was not what God wanted. By removing all yeasts by burning with fire symbolized that they were completely liberated from the old life by leaving Egypt.

Rabbis teach that just as leaven makes bread swollen, so it makes a human being proud. They also teach that un-swollen bread means humility, obedience, and the will to remove the tendency of sin inside human beings. Consequently, the Exodus alone was not perfect or sufficient. It is because God liberated the Israelites from Egypt not for only their physical freedom, but also for freedom from the shackles of sin.[10]

Historical Accomplishment

Just as the lamb of Passover was accomplished through the passion and death of Jesus Christ, so the Festival of Unleavened Bread was accomplished through the suffering and tomb of Jesus Christ. If so, let us study how the Festival of Unleavened Bread was historically accomplished through Jesus Christ. Regarding this study, we will learn about the following three aspects: first, offering; second, bread; and third, leaven.

Offering

Just as death of the lamb of Passover was accomplished through Jesus Christ, so the offering of the Festival of Unleavened Bread

---

9. Howard & Rosenthal, *The Festivals of the Lord*, 68.
10. Williams, *The Holidays of God: Spring Festivals*, 16.

was accomplished through Jesus Christ. During the Festival of Unleavened Bread, just as a bull, a ram, and a male goat, along with the cereal offering became the offering by fire every day, so Jesus Christ became an offering by fire. Jesus was interrogated all night long. He was also whipped, and his body was smeared with blood so no one could recognize His semblance. The prophecy of a Hebrew prophet was fulfilled: *As many were astonished at him–his appearance was so marred, beyond human semblance, and his form beyond that of the sons of men* (Isaiah 52:14).

This was insufficient so the Israelites hung Jesus on the cross for six hours. This picture was as prophesized long before. The author of Psalms described it as follows:

> Yea, dogs are round about me; a company of evildoers encircle me; they have pierced my hands and feet—I can count all my bones – they stare and gloat over me; they divide my garments among them, and for my raiment they cast lots (Psalms 22:16-18).

The pain of dying on the cross, literally, can only be the accomplishment of an offering by fire at the Festival of Unleavened Bread.

The picture that Jesus was being hung on the cross was the representation of a bull, lamb, and male goat that were killed as offerings. John expresses it in another way: *So the soldiers... when they came to Jesus and saw that he was already dead, they did not break his legs. But one of the soldiers pierced his side with a spear, and at once there came out blood and water* (John 19:32-34). Being pierced was also as prophesized earlier: *They look on him whom they have pierced...*(Zechariah 12:10). *Someday, they will directly come to see the one who was pierced so* (Revelation 1:7).

At last, when Jesus breathed out His last breath, the soldiers of Rome tied His body like a mummy and threw it into a tomb. They closed the tomb with a stone door (Matthew 27:59-60). According to an old document, this stone door was so large that at least twenty men were needed to roll it away.[11] Also, a Roman seal was placed on the stone door. Jesus Christ was buried so, bearing all

---

11. Booker, *Celebrating Jesus in the Biblical Festivals*, 74.

sins, sufferings, diseases, and deaths of human beings. In this way, Jesus became the protagonist of the Festival of Unleavened Bread.

Bread

According to the teachings of rabbis, in order for unleavened bread to be seen as marred, the Israelites baked it by hitting, piercing, and burning.[12] This was not an accidental happening. Through the experience and tradition of Israel, God fulfilled the prophecy of a Jewish prophet: *He was wounded for our transgressions, he was bruised for our iniquities; upon him was the chastisement that made us whole, and with his stripes we are healed* (Isaiah 53:5).

Indicating that He Himself is such bread, Jesus Christ said, "who eats this bread will receive eternal life":

> So Jesus said to them… unless you eat the flesh of the Son of man and drink his blood, you have no life in you; he who eats my flesh and drinks my blood has eternal life, and I will raise him up at the last day. For my flesh is food indeed, and my blood is drink indeed. He who eats my flesh and drinks my blood abides in me, and I in him… so he who eats me will live because of me (John 6:53-57).

Through this saying, Jesus Christ teaches that His becoming like unleavened bread allows for human beings to accept Him. This invitation is similar to the time when they left Egypt; the Israelites left with only unleavened bread, so when we come to Jesus Christ, we should throw away our old nature and way of life in order to resemble His nature. This is an invitation to quit the old way of life. It is a lesson that when we leave "Egypt," we should throw away what should be thrown away and take what should be taken.

In review, why should the Israelites eat unleavened bread for seven days during the Festival of Unleavened Bread? For two reasons! The first reason is in order for the Israelites to become holy people, even though it is only for seven days. Second, it is in order for them to walk with the Lord in holiness. These are the same reasons for us Christians. Just as the Israelites who experienced redemption from the shackles of sin through the lamb of Passover, so should Christians live clean and holy lives through Jesus Christ

---

12. Williams, *The Holidays of God: Spring Festivals*, 17.

every day, being the unleavened bread of the Festival of Unleavened Bread.[13]

Leaven

Jesus Christ was like bread made without **leaven**. Leaven symbolizes one's old nature or sin. However, as already mentioned, no sin was found in Jesus. Distributing to his disciples unleavened bread to symbolize His body without sin, Jesus said: *This is my body which is given for you. Do this in remembrance of me* (Luke 22:19; 1 Corinthians 11:24). Serving a similar purpose as the unleavened bread, He offered His body for others.

Jesus Christ had no leaven, but became bread with leaven by taking all of our leavens. That is why Jewish people removed His body as soon as He died on the cross. Only after they removed the leaven, could they participate in Passover and the Festival of Unleavened Bread. Just as the Jewish people removed physical leaven, so does Christ want us to remove the spiritual leaven from within us and our homes. He took the leaven of our sin to His spirit, leaven of our sorrows to His soul, and the leaven of our disease and death to His body.[14]

A Jewish scholar Paul, who understood the meaning of the Festival of Unleavened Bread in the Old Testament and the New, advised Christians as follows:

> Cleanse out the old leaven that you may be a new lump, as you really are unleavened. For Christ, our paschal lamb, has been sacrificed. Let us, therefore, celebrate the festival, not with the old leaven, the leaven of malice and evil, but with the unleavened bread of sincerity and truth (1 Corinthians 5: 7-8).

Jesus Christ, the protagonist of the Festival of Unleavened Bread, has given the purpose of a new life.

Jesus Christ who had no leaven became leaven for us. By being taken hastily into a tomb, Jesus Christ was abandoned like bread of

---

13. Francis, *Celebrate the Festivals of the Lord*, 34-5.
14. Booker, *Celebrating Jesus in the Biblical Festivals*, 73.

the Festival of Unleavened Bread. He was buried in the tomb, taking our leaven, where all of our leavens were also buried with Him. The vestiges of our old nature, suppression, oppression, sorrows, and suffering were buried in the tomb with Him. He took the debt of all sins that human beings suffer.

A poem beautifully describes this aspect of Jesus Christ. Let us sing of His new appearance:

> O Thou, the Lamb of God, spotless and most holy, is slain. Th'unblemish'd Lamb, to bear our sins at Calvary. This is the broken body, The body marr'd for me, The very body of the Lord, Nail-broken on the tree. This is the blood outpour'd, In judgment, in my stead; For you, for me at Calvary In love and mercy shed. Here is the table spread Which Jesus doth prepare, Who gives us now this bread of life, 'This cup which now we share. The Lord for Whom we yearn, ascended for a space, Comes soon, and we at His return With joy shall see His face. And we? Until that hour, let us, in ev'ry place Bear still our cross, still tell His pow'r, His mercy and His grace![15]

As in this hymn, we should become believers who wait for His Second Advent, sharing Jesus Christ who was marred on the cross and abandoned to a tomb.

---

15. Korean-English Hymnal 281

Chapter 6

The First Fruits

As mentioned several times before, the Festival of First Fruits combined with Passover and the Festival of Unleavened Bread make the festivals of spring, with the Festival of First Fruits being the last. According to the date, we can easily see that these three festivals go together. According to the sacred calendar, the date of Passover is Nissan 14, and the Festival of Unleavened Bread starts the next day, day 15, and lasts to day 21. Since the Festival of First Fruits is required to be kept on the day after the Sabbath, its first day is the 16th of Nissan (Leviticus 23:11). So, the first grain was offered on the second day of the Festival of Unleavened Bread.

Biblical Background

In order to study the biblical background of the Festival of First Fruits, the third festival of the seven festivals of the Israelites, let us read the Word of God[1]:

> The Lord said to Moses, "Speak to the Israelites and say to them: 'When you enter the land I am going to give you and you reap its harvest, bring to the priest a sheaf of **the first grain** you harvest. He is to wave the sheaf before the Lord so it will be accepted on your behalf; the priest is to wave it on the day after the Sabbath. On the day you wave the sheaf, you must sacrifice as a burnt offering to the Lord a lamb a year old without defect, together with its

---

1. The Festival of First Fruits is called *Ha Bikkurim* (הבכורים) in Hebrew.

grain offering of two-tenths of an ephah of fine flour mixed with oil—an offering made to the Lord by fire, a pleasing aroma— and its drink offering of a quarter of a hin of wine. You must not eat any bread, or roasted or new grain, until the very day you bring this offering to your God. This is to be a lasting ordinance for the generations to come, wherever you live (Leviticus 23:9-14).

The Festival of First Fruits is distinct from both Passover and the Festival of Unleavened Bread in that both were kept while the Israelites were in Egypt, while the Festival of First Fruits was kept after the Israelites entered the land God had promised to them. The reason for this is simple! They could not engage in agriculture until after entering the Promised Land. The group was moving incessantly in the wilderness toward their destination. One cannot farm while on the move!

After entering the Promised Land Canaan, the Israelites engaged in farming, and the first production of a year was always barley. When they harvested the barley in the spring that they had planted as seed in winter, the Israelites brought the first sheaf to the temple as an offering of thanks to God for allowing the harvest. Since the harvest of the barley was the first product of the year, it represented all products during a year. Therefore, an abundant harvest of barley symbolized God's blessing upon the remainder of the harvest.[2]

According to the Word of God, in the Festival of First Fruits the Israelites were required to bring a sheaf to the temple, which the priest waved in order that God would accept it. When they offered a sheaf of the first grain, they also had to offer the following: a year old male lamb without blemish as the burnt offering, wine as the drink offering, and fine flour mixed with oil as the cereal offering. Also, the Israelites were not to eat any of the products until they offered the first grain[3] (Leviticus 23:14).

---

2. Howard & Rosenthal, *The Festivals of the Lord*, 75.

3. The reason that they could not eat the products until they offered the First Fruits is as follows: Since God is the owner of the land, and they are the children of the Lord, the first harvest, that is, the best should be given to God. John E. Hartly, *Leviticus, Word Biblical Commentary*, vol. 4, ed. Glenn W. Barke (Dallas, TX: Word Books, Publisher, 1992), 386.

After He accepted the sheaf of the first grain, God gave it back to the priests and the Levites, who served in the temple, as their daily food. God took the responsibility for the life of those who committed for Him. God clearly mentioned this in the following text: *The Levitical priests, that is, all the tribe of Levi, shall have no portion or inheritance with Israel; they shall at the offerings by fire to the Lord, and his rightful dues* (Deuteronomy 18:1).

God specially cared for the priests of the Levites because they were the mediators between God and the Israelites. So, God described the food in detail so the priests would be assured they were adequately supplied:

> This shall be the priests' due from the people, from those offering a sacrifice, whether it be ox or sheep: they shall give to the priest the shoulder and the two cheeks and the stomach. The first fruits of your grain, of your wine and of your oil, and the first of the fleece of your sheep, you shall give him (Deuteronomy 18:3-4).

God also instructed in detail the method by which to offer the First Fruits after the Israelites entered Canaan. The explanation is as follows:

> When you come into the land which the Lord your God gives you for an inheritance, and have taken possession of it, and live in it, you shall take some of the first of all the fruit of the ground, which you harvest from your land that the Lord your God gives you, and you shall put it in a basket, and you shall go to the place which the Lord your God will choose, to make his name to dwell there (Deuteronomy 26:1-2).

The Israelites came to the temple and gave the first grain to the priest. They gave this first product of harvest to him while confessing their faith, as follows: I *declare this day to the Lord your God that I have come into the land, which the Lord swore to our fathers to give us* (Deuteronomy 26:3). Then the priest took the basket from their hands, and set it down before the altar of God (Deuteronomy 26:4).

When the priest finished setting down the basket before the altar, in accordance with the commandment of God, the Israelites recited the following Word of God in front of the priest:

Then you shall declare before the Lord your God: "My father was a wandering Aramean, and he went down into Egypt with a few people and lived there and became a great nation, powerful and numerous. But the Egyptians mistreated us and made us suffer, putting us to hard labor. Then we cried out to the Lord, the God of our fathers, and the Lord heard our voice and saw our misery, toil and oppression. So the Lord brought us out of Egypt with a mighty hand and an outstretched arm, with great terror and with miraculous signs and wonders. He brought us to this place and gave us this land, a land flowing with milk and honey; and now I bring the First Fruits of the soil that you, O Lord, have given me." Place the basket before the Lord your God and bow down before him (Deuteronomy 26:5-10).

To recite the Word of God like this was part of the service of the Festival of First Fruits, but it was not a simple service. The Israelites remembered and thanked God for His grace to have delivered them from the status of slaves in order to establish a new and independent country. In particular, through the Festival of First Fruits, they confessed that the foundation of all things was Almighty God who had given the products to them as the gift of grace and they thanked Him for their ability to come and offer the first grain as free men and women, not as slaves.[4]

Service of the Festival of First Fruits

The Israelites regarded the Festival of First Fruits as important, and therefore, they shared their joy of keeping the festival for the nation and for the family. Let us look at how they inaugurated the service of offering with the priest on behalf of the nation.

For the Nation

After choosing the place to plant, the Israelites planted barley that would become an offering of the first grain. The place that they chose was in an area known as the Ashes Valley, and it was a small field across the Kidron alongside with Jerusalem. Green slopes lay in the background, and the place was full of olive trees. This place

---

4. Williams, *The Holidays of God: Spring Festivals*, 22.

was a special field, cultivated solely for the national First Fruits offering.⁵

The Israelites plowed the field in the autumn and planted barley in winter. Constantly overseeing the field, overseers observed that barley in the field grew naturally. The reason was simple! Since the barley to be offered to God was raised by God, they did not do any artificial watering or fertilization. As the spring came after winter, the field began to change to yellow. At the advent of the Festival of First Fruits, the representatives of the Sanhedrin came to the field, selected some sheaves, and marked them.

At sunset on Nissan 15, three priests from the Sanhedrin emerged from the temple, and excited observers gathered. They went to the field to reap the First Fruits. With sickles in hand and baskets under their arms, the three men went to the place of the already marked sheaves of barley. At the moment of reaping all people closed their mouths and were quiet; solemnity reigned. Suddenly, the three priests broke the stillness with a series of questions to the onlookers:

> Has the sun set?
> With this sickle?
> Into this basket?
> On this Sabbath?
> Shall I reap?

The onlookers responded "yes" to those questions. After repeating the questions two times, the priests began to reap the marked sheaves. They reaped until one ephah of barley, that is, one omer was obtained.⁶ Then they took them to the temple. The grain was threshed with rods. It was then parched over an open flame and winnowed in the wind to remove the chaff.

Next, the barley was milled until it became very fine flour. According to the Talmud, it was milled until the inspector could plunge his hands into the flour and remove them without any flour adhering to his hands. On Nisan 16, the flour was presented to God.

---

5. Howard & Rosenthal, *The Festivals of the Lord*, 78. The following content, as a whole, refers to this book.

6. An omer is about two liters.

After the flour was mixed with olive oil and a small amount of frankincense was sprinkled upon it, the priest waved it before God. A small amount was burned, and the remainder was given to the Levites.

For the Family

First Fruits was a national observance, but each family also observed it. Each family brought First Fruits to the temple. In early spring, Israelite farmers performed the service of setting their First Fruits apart. Farmers went to the field with the skipping children and marked the best of their unripened crops. The marked crops were tied in order not to be damaged. Then, farmers declared: "Behold, these are the First Fruits!" They enjoyed watching as the marked First Fruits ripened. Then, they made a pilgrimage to Jerusalem with the harvest. Finally, Nisan 16 arrived. Outside the gates of the temple, farmers joyfully replied, responding to the haunting melody of flutes: *Praise God in His sanctuary!* (Psalms 150:1). Inside the temple gates, Levitical choirs led the music with Psalms 30:

> *I will extol thee, O Lord, for thou hast drawn me up, and hast not let my foes rejoice over me...*
> *As entering the temple of God, many farmers also praised like this:*
> *Let everything that has breath praise the Lord!*

Of course, everyone could sing this song. When the priest stepped toward the people to receive the First Fruits, farmers prayed the prayer of the First Fruits with resounding voices:

> *I declare this day to the Lord your God that I have come into the land which the Lord swore to our fathers to give us* (Deuteronomy 26:3).

Farmers then removed the baskets from their shoulders and handed them to the priest. In the simple baskets made of peeled willow shoots lay one sheaf of barley, that is, one omer. The priest placed his hands under each basket and slowly waved it before

God. Next the farmers recited loudly from Deuteronomy 26:5, 9-10:

> *A wandering Aramean was my father; and he went down into Egypt and sojourned there... there he became a nation, great, mighty, and populous... he brought us into this place... I bring the first of the fruit of the ground.*

With the thanksgiving prayer complete, the priest set the basket in front of the altar and cast a handful of the grain upon the fire. Farmers fell on their faces to worship God and then returned to the outer court where the family waited for them. Rejoicing, the family clutched the father's knees. By this, they kept the Festival of First Fruits with an attitude of holiness. They returned to their homes, praising the Lord, who faithfully gave the harvest.

First Fruits in a Narrow Meaning

In the New Testament, the word of the first grain or First Fruits occurs eight times. Two of them indicate Jesus Christ, and the remaining six indicate Christians. The First Fruits indicating Christ means His resurrection. While barley is buried in the soil as if it dies during cold winter, it resurrects as a bud in spring. Just as they set aside the first grain of this resurrected barley and presented it to God, so Jesus Christ rose on the third day after He died and was sanctified to God (Romans 1:4).

The Apostle Paul's declaration that Jesus Christ became the First Fruits by resurrecting after he died reads as follows: *But in fact Christ has been raised from the dead, the first fruits of those who have fallen asleep* (1 Corinthians 15:20). According to this saying, the resurrected Jesus Christ is the First Fruits of those who have fallen asleep. As mentioned above, the First Fruits represent all harvests to be reaped in the future. Therefore, Jesus Christ is the one who resurrected for the first time among all those who will be raised.[7]

---

7. Anthony C. Thiselton, *The First Epistle to the Corinthians* (Grand Rapids, MI: Williams B. Eerdmans Publishing House, 2000), 1224.

In other words, it is as follows: since Jesus Christ rose for the first time among those who had fallen asleep, that is, those who had died, others also will arise someday. Since the first product means the best one, the remaining products are the same kind as Jesus Christ, but they may not be as good as the first product.[8] However, since the remainder necessarily follows the first product, all others must rise. It means Jesus Christ arose for the first time among them.

To complement this content, Paul additionally says: *Each in his own order: Christ the first fruits, then at his coming those who belong to Christ. Then comes the end, when he delivers the kingdom to God the Father after destroying every rule and every authority and power* (1 Corinthians 15:23-24). According to this saying, two kinds of people will rise again after Christ: first, at His Second Coming, the Christians who belong to Christ; second, will be the unbelievers who will be arisen in order to receive the final judgment.

These unbelievers are those who rejected Jesus Christ. In other words, they are the power that made human beings fight against God.[9] They will also live again as an eternal body and come to receive the eternal judgment. Jesus Himself mentioned this: *And come forth, those who have done good, to the resurrection of life, and those who have done evil, to the resurrection of judgment* (John 5:29). Of course, here doing good means the act of believing to accept God's Son Jesus Christ as the Savior of God's good will (Cf. John 6:29).

When did Jesus Christ arise? According to Leviticus, the Festival of First Fruits was the next day after the Sabbath (Leviticus 23:11). Jesus Christ, the first grain in the New Testament, also rose on the next day after the Sabbath. The Bible says about the day: Now after the Sabbath, toward the dawn of the first day of the week, Mary Magdalene and the other Mary went to see the sepul-

---

8. Ibid., 1223.
9. Frederic Louis Godet, *Commentary on First Corinthians* (Grand Rapids, MI: Kregal Publications, 1977), 788.

cher (Matthew 28:1). Yes! He arose on the Lord's Day as recorded in Leviticus, not on just any day.

To look again at the death and resurrection of Jesus Christ in light of Leviticus is beneficial. Jesus kept the Passover with His disciples on Nisan 14 and died on the cross. On Nisan 15, that is, on the day of Preparation, He was buried in a tomb:

> And when evening had come, since it was the day of Preparation, that is, the day before the Sabbath, Joseph of Arimathea, a respected member of the council, who was also himself looking for the kingdom of God, took courage and went to Pilate, and asked for the body of Jesus (Mark 15:42-43).

Nisan 15 is the Festival of Unleavened Bread, which is also Saturday. Jesus Christ endured all kinds of suffering and death and was finally buried in the cruel tomb. However, since He took the sin and judgment of human beings, Jesus Christ could not stay in the tomb. He arose to declare that the sin of human beings was forgiven (Romans 4:25). His resurrection was the historical event that happened on Nisan 16, that is, on the Festival of First Fruits.[10]

When many people were joyful and singing, presenting the offering of the first grain in the temple, Jesus Christ arose breaking the wall of death. When the priests were waving the offering of the first grain from top to bottom before God, Jesus Christ rose from bottom to top. He was the first sheaf of barley who was truly arisen among the dead. Not only this! Just as the priests waved the offering, Jesus Christ ascended and presented Himself to God as the First Fruits of the resurrection.[11]

First Fruits in a Broad Meaning

God did not call only Jesus Christ to be the First Fruits. Besides Christ, there were others who were called the First Fruits. The Israelites were one group. Through Jeremiah, let us read the Word in which God called the Israelites His First Fruits: *Israel was holy to the LORD, the first fruits of his harvest* (2:3). How did the Israel-

---

10. Francis, *Celebrate the Festivals of the Lord*, 46-47.
11. Booker, *Celebrating Jesus in the Biblical Festivals*, 85.

ites become the First Fruits of God? An answer can be found in the Passover.

Right before the Israelites experienced the Exodus, all eldest sons and animals were under the curse of death and judgment.[12] The only method of escape from the curse was through the blood of the lamb without blemish of Passover. They had to believe in God who proposed the method of death and blood and exercise the belief into action. By killing the lamb of Passover instead of their eldest sons and by striking its blood on the door, the Israelites could not only escape death, but also experience the Exodus (Exodus 12:12-13).

After this, since God saved them with His method, the eldest sons of Israel and the first young of all animals then belonged to God (Exodus 34:19). The eldest son represented the whole family, and the first young of an animal represented the whole of animals. For this reason, God could declare that Israel was the First Fruits of His products. However, by grace, God required only the first sons, the representatives of the family. *The first-born of your sons you shall give to me* (Exodus 22:29).

In fact, since God is the Creator of all products, they all belong to God. However, God requested only the First Fruits as in the case of the eldest sons among all products. Let us read the Word of God: *The best of the first fruits of your ground you shall bring into the house of the Lord your God* (Exodus 23:19). This principle was also applied to the seven important agricultural products from land—barley, wheat, grapes, figs, pomegranates, olives, and honey (Deuteronomy 8:8).

The expression of the First Fruits occurs eight times in the New Testament. Two of them, as mentioned above, indicate the resurrection of Jesus Christ. Keeping in mind the fact that the important agricultural products are seven kinds, it can be said that the expression of the First Fruits in the New Testament is of seven kinds. Matthew records the fact that when Jesus Christ rose, many believers rose together. These beliers are just like some stalks of barley tied together in order to make a sheaf when the Israelites presented a sheaf of the first grain of barley in the Old Testament.

---

12. Howard & Rosenthal, *The Festivals of the Lord*, 84.

Likewise, when Jesus Christ rose as the First Fruits, many stalks, that is, many believers were tied together and offered to God.[13] Let us see the Word that clearly proposes this fact: *the tombs also were opened, and many bodies of the saints who had fallen asleep were raised, and coming out of the tombs after his resurrection they went into the holy city and appeared to many* (Matthew 27:52-53). Since God accepted Jesus Christ, the First Fruits of this resurrection, He also accepted the believers who became the sheaf along with Jesus.

The Apostle Paul said that lovely Epaenetus is ***the First Fruits of Achaia unto Christ*** (Romans 16:5, KJV). Like this, First Fruits is applicable not only to an individual, but also to a family. Paul said to the Church of Corinthians to respect and obey the household of Stephanas: *Brethren, the house of Stephanas, that it is the First Fruits of Achaia, and [that] they have addicted themselves to the ministry of the saints, That ye submit yourselves unto such, and to everyone that helpeth with [us], and laboureth* (1 Corinthians 16:15-16, KJV).

How did these people become the First Fruits in Christ? The process was due to the roots of the fruits. Let us read the words of Paul: *If the dough offered as **first fruits** is holy, so is the whole lump; and if the root is holy, so are the branches* (Romans 11:16). From this saying, the phrase of "if the dough offered as First Fruits" means that since He accepted the forefathers of Israel, that is, Abraham, Isaac, and Jacob, as the First Fruits, God also accepts the believers who are grafted onto them by faith.[14]

So, how did Christians become the First Fruits of resurrection? God accepted them as the First Fruits by His use of two methods. The first method was **the Word of truth**. Following is the explanation of James: *Of his own will he brought us forth by the word of truth that we should be a kind of first fruits of his creatures* (James 1:18). The Word of power causes Christians to have become the fruits of resurrection with Christ (Cf. 1 Peter 1:23).

The second method was **the work of the Holy Spirit**. Let us study the method the Apostle Paul suggested: Not only the creation,

---

13. Booker, *Celebrating Jesus in the Biblical Festivals*, 86.
14. Howard & Rosenthal, *The Festivals of the Lord*, 85.

but we ourselves, who have **the first fruits** of the Spirit, groan inwardly as we wait for adoption as sons, the redemption of our bodies (Romans 8:23). The Holy Spirit dwells in the lives of the believers, the fruits of resurrection. The Holy Spirit guarantees that one day, at His second Coming, their limited bodies will be changed to imperishable, holy, and glorious bodies (Ephesians 1:14).

The Israelites are the last people to which the expression of the First Fruits is applied in the New Testament. With 12,000 from each tribe, 144,000 in total were described as the First Fruits (Revelation 14). Let us figure the attributes of such people from the Word of God: It is these who have not defiled themselves with women, for they are chaste; it is these who follow the Lamb wherever he goes; these have been redeemed from mankind as **first fruits** for God and the Lamb (Revelation 14:4).

Why are these people the First Fruits? They are the first fruits because of their status and work. At His Second Coming, the Church will be lifted up and no longer exist on earth. While all people are in the day of trouble, 144,000 of Israel will reap the harvest among the Israelites. They will urge the remaining people of Israel to repent and lead them to Jesus Christ. They will harvest many as First Fruits.[15]

---

15. Ibid., 85-86.

Chapter 7

Waiting for Pentecost

Thus far, we have looked at the festivals of spring; Passover, the Festival of Unleavened Bread, and the Festival of First Fruits. Passover was connected to the death of Jesus Christ, and the Festival of Unleavened Bread was connected to the suffering and tomb of Jesus. While these two negative festivals, the Festival of First Fruits was a positive one in that it was connected to Jesus Christ, the First Fruits of resurrection. By rising again on the third after His death, He gave new hope to human beings who are doomed to die.

The Festival of First Fruits is an important festival in determining the date of the Festival of Pentecost. In other words, the Israelites must count the days from the date that they presented the barley at the Festival of First Fruits, to the Festival of Pentecost. For this reason, the Festival of First Fruits is closely connected to the Festival of Pentecost. In order to see this connection, let us return to the Bible:

> You shall also count for yourselves from the day after the sabbath, from the day when you brought in the sheaf of the wave offering; there shall be seven complete sabbaths. You shall count fifty days to the day after the seventh sabbath; then you shall present a new grain offering to the LORD (Leviticus 23:15-16, NASB).

According to the above passage, the Israelites should begin to count fifty days from the day that they bring an offering of the first grain to be waved (the method of presentation to God) by the priest. Why?

The reason is simple! First of all, God said, "there shall be seven complete Sabbaths," which means to count forty nine days. One week is seven days from the Lord's Day to Saturday so the commandment to count seven Sabbaths is to continue to count the number of days until the Sabbath passes seven times. To count the next day of the seventh Sabbath after completing forty nine days, the number finally becomes fifty days.

In fact, Pentecost means fifty, and so the festival of Pentecost is the festival of 50 literally. Therefore, the Pentecost falls on the fiftieth day from the Festival of First Fruits. That is why Pentecost is also called the Festival of Weeks used for emphasizing the passing of seven weeks from the Festival of First Fruits (Exodus 34:22). It is also called the Festival of Harvest because it is the festival for which wheat is harvested.

The Israelites call the event of counting these important days ***spirat haomer*** (תרפס מעהר). ***Spirat***, which means "counting" or "fathoming," and ***haomer*** means sheaf. (Since *Ha* is the article in Hebrew, it has no meaning.) Therefore, to interpret this, it is counting the **omer**. By the way, **omer** is an interesting word because it has two meanings.

Originally, **omer** meant a unit of measure of volume, and it means a tenth ephah or a volume of two liters (Exodus 16:36). It was translated to also mean a sheaf in the Bible. Therefore, **omer** can be either a unit of measure of volume, or a sheaf. It is all translated to mean a sheaf in Leviticus 23:10, 11, 12, and 15. Let us study one of them: *Say to the Israelites, When you come into the land which I give you and reap its harvest, you shall bring the **sheaf** of the first fruits of your harvest to the priest* (Leviticus 23:10).

Counting the Omer

To translate *omer* is difficult because **omer** has always had a double meaning. The writer will use **omer** as in the original language.[1] The Israelites should count the number of days everyday from the day that the priest presented an **omer** of the first grain of barley to God by waving it, until the Pentecost. For this reason, the counting act is counting the **omer**. The Israelites do this counting of the **omer** in accordance with rules, not at their discretion.[2]

The Israelites start counting the **omer** in the evening, that is, when a new day begins for them. First of all, the parent reads the Word of God:

> And you shall count from the morrow after the Sabbath... seven full weeks shall they be, counting fifty days to the morrow after the seventh Sabbath; then you shall present a cereal offering of new grain to the Lord (Leviticus 23:15-16).

Then, the whole family says:
"This is the first day of the **omer**."

Then they read the Psalms that falls to the day (Appendix 1).
Then they mark the date on the chart (Appendix 2).
They pray this counting of the **omer**:

> May it be Your will, Lord our God, and the God of our forefathers, that in the merit of the omer count that I have counted today, may there be corrected whatever blemish I have caused...and may be cleansed and sanctified with the holiness of Above.[3]

Lastly, they end with the following prayer:

> We praise you, O Lord our God, King of the Universe, who has given us commandments to obey. It is our desire to be obedient to

---

1. Noordtzij also calls it omer thinking of the double meaning. Noordtzij, *Bible Student's Commentary*: Levticus, 23.

2. About the rules, see the book, Zimmerman, *Celebrating Biblical Festivals*, 103 ff.

3. *Shavuot-Its Observance, Laws and Significance* (Brooklyn, NY: Mesorah Publication, Ltd., 1997), 35. Williams, *The Holidays of God: Spring Festivals*, 24.

Your laws, knowing that they will enable us to live in a right relationship with you and with each other. Thank You for picking us up when we stumble over stones and for sending Your Holy Spirit to comfort us!4

The same service is practiced on the next day. Only the day is different. On the second day, they say the next line: "This is the second day of the **omer**." On the third day, they say: "This is the third day of the **omer**." On the tenth day, they say this: "This is the tenth day of the **omer**." Counting the number of days every day, they continue this practice at home (or in synagogue) until Pentecost.

In looking at the prayer that the Israelites prayed we see they had a sincere wish to wait for the Pentecost, but they also focused on reflecting about their everyday lives. Doing so, they expected a great work that God would accomplish on the fiftieth day after the day that they offered the First Fruits on Pentecost. During this period that counts the omer, as if they wait for a good friend, their sincere desire to wait for a new festival of God is expressed.

In the New Testament

In light of the New Testament, the Pentecost means the period of fifty days from the resurrection of Jesus Christ until the Coming of the Holy Spirit. This period is divided again into two segments: forty days and ten days. The first forty days, Jesus Christ spent with His disciples and other people with whom He was intimate on earth. And the last ten days are the period after Jesus Christ ascended to God. On the fiftieth day, He received the Holy Spirit from God and sent the Spirit to 120 believers.

The Apostle Peter, who experienced being filled with the Holy Spirit at the Pentecost, described well this process, that is, Jesus rose again, ascended, and sent the Holy Spirit: *This Jesus God raised up, and of that we all are witnesses. Being therefore exalted at the right hand of God, and having received from the Father the promise of the Holy Spirit, he has poured out this which you see and hear* (Acts 2:32-33).

---

4. Zimmerman, *Celebrating Biblical Festivals*, 103.

While the period of fifty days for His disciples was the time of grace on the one hand, it was also the time of waiting, on the other hand. The period of the time of grace was because Jesus Christ, who died on the cross as if He had abandoned them, rose from the dead. The period was also a time of waiting because there was a promise that the resurrected Christ promised many times. The promise was that the disciples would receive the promise of God, that is, the indwelling and the fullness of the Holy Spirit (Luke 24:49; Acts 1:5).

Just as the Israelites waited for fifty days, counting every day and just as the disciples of Jesus waited for fifty days, we Christians need to wait for a similar time. Just as the disciples waited, reflecting on themselves (Acts 1:16 ff), so we should wait, reflecting on ourselves. Also, just as the disciples prayed with all their hearts while waiting (Acts 1:14) and were finally filled with the Holy Spirit (Acts 2:4), we should be praying to be filled with the Holy Spirit.

While He stayed on earth for forty days after He arose, in other words, before He ascended, Jesus Christ frequently told the disciples to wait. However, He also gave important teachings for the period. The first important teaching was the fact that they, on behalf of the Lord, would be sent out into the earth world: *As the Father has sent me, even so I send you* (John 20:21).

In other words, it was this enormous teaching that from that point forward, the disciples should spread the gospel on behalf of their Lord, Jesus Christ.[5] This teaching that the resurrected Lord first gave the disciples was absolutely impossible from the human perspective. Jesus, who knew well such a fact, said to them *to be filled with Holy Spirit* (John 20:21).

---

5. That the Lord gave the disciples the Holy Spirit is a turning point in three aspects: First, the ministry of the Lord was changed to that of the disciples through the Holy Spirit; second, the human limitation was overcome through the Holy Spirit; and third, the salvation of sinners was realized through the ministry of the Holy Spirit. John Sungchul Hong, *Junimeu JisangMyeongryeong: Seonggyeong Uimiwa Jeokyong* (*The GreatCommission of the Lord: Biblical Meaning and Application*) (Seoul: Saebok Publishing House, 2004), 29.

Yes! The Lord taught the fact that the evangelization of the world was absolutely impossible through only their power, but would be accomplished through the indwelling and work of the Holy Spirit, and He gave the Holy Spirit as a gift in order to make them experience the Holy Spirit. If it were not for this experience, they might not have obeyed the Lord's commandment of *I send the promise of my Father upon you; but stay in the city, until you are clothed with power from on high* (Luke 24:49; Acts 1:4).

Jesus Christ then taught in detail to the disciples the important things about the evangelization of the world. For example, in the gospel of Matthew, He commanded, *Go therefore and make disciples of all nations* (Matthew 28:19). In another teaching, He informed them of the fact that these ministries are impossible without depending on the power of the Holy Spirit (Acts 1:8).

Just as the Israelites had the Pentecost, with their cleansing and counting of fifty days with the full expectation after the Festival of First Fruits, so the disciples reflected on themselves and waited, praying with the same full expectation. Jesus Christ, the Paschal lamb and the protagonist of the Festival of Unleavened Bread became the firstfruit of resurrection and let the disciples know to wait for the next festival, or, the Pentecost when they would be filled with the Holy Spirit.

Appendix I*

The following Psalms are the Word to read counting the **omer**.

Day	Description	Psalms
1	The Law of the Lord	119:1-8
2	Obedience to the Law of the Lord	119:9-16
3	Happiness in the Law of the Lord	119:17-24
4	Determination to obey the Law of the Lord	119:25-32
5	A prayer for understanding	119:33-40
6	Trusting the Law of the Lord	119:41-48
7	Confidence in the Law of the Lord	119:49-56
8	Devotion to the Law of the Lord	119:57-64
9	The value of the Law of the Lord	119:65-72
10	The justice of the Law of the Lord	119:73-80
11	Prayer for deliverance	119:81-88
12	Faith in the Law of the Lord	119:89-96
13	Love for the Law of the Lord	119:97-104
14	Light from the Law of the Lord	119:105-112
15	Safety in the Law of the Lord	119:113-120
16	Obedience to the Law of the Lord	119:121-128
17	Desire to obey the Law of the Lord	119:129-136
18	The justice of the Law of the Lord	119:137-144
19	Prayer for deliverance	119:145-152
20	Plea for salvation	119:153-160
21	Dedication to the Law of the Lord	119:161-168
22	A prayer for help	119:169-176
23	True happiness	1:1-6
24	Confidence in the Lord	11:1-7
25	What God requires	15:1-5
26	The Law of the Lord	19:7-14
27	A prayer for guidance	25:4-10
28	Longing for God	63:1-8
29	A song of thanksgiving	67:1-7
30	God and His people	78:1-16

31	God and His people	78:17-31
32	God and His people	78:32-39
33	God and His people	78:40-55
34	God and His people	78:56-72
35	God the King	93:1-5
36	God the Judge	94:12-23
37	A song of praise	95:1-7
38	God the Supreme King	96:1-13
39	God the Ruler of the World	98:1-9
40	God the Supreme King	99:1-9
41	The love of God	103:1-22
42	God and His people	105:1-11
43	The Lord's goodness	106:1-5
44	In praise of the Lord	111:1-10
45	The happiness of a good person	112:1-10
46	The reward of obedience	128:1-6
47	A prayer for help	130:1-8
48	A call for the universe to praise God	148:1-14
49	A prayer of thanksgiving	138:1-8
50	Praise the Lord	150:1-6

*This appendix is adapted from Zimmerman, *Celebrating Biblical Festivals*, 103-5.

Appendix II*

Whenever the **omer** is counted, one of the family marks X on the day.

First Day X						

*This appendix is adapted from Zimmerman, *Celebrating Biblical Festivals*, 102

Chapter 8

The Pentecost

Pentecost is one of the three festival seasons of Israel, along with Passover and the Festival of Tabernacles. The Pentecost originating from the Greek means fifty days.[1] As already mentioned, this means the fiftieth day from the day that the first grain (First Fruits) was offered is the Pentecost. Though introduced in Leviticus 23: 15-16, the name of the festival is not mentioned: *And you shall count from the morrow after the Sabbath, from the day that you brought the sheaf of the wave offering; seven full weeks shall they be, counting **fifty days** to the morrow after the seventh Sabbath.*

The Festival of First Fruits grain offering was barley, but the offering presented after fifty days was wheat, because wheat was the first harvest of early summer. For this reason, the Israelites called it "the festival of the harvest" or the festival of the harvest of wheat. However, the Bible implies that the wheat was the first product: *You shall keep the festival of harvest, of the first fruits of your labor, of what you sow in the field* (Exodus 23:16).[2]

Pentecost is known by a variety of names. As mentioned above, since the First Fruits of wheat is offered in the Pentecost, it is also

---

1. The Pentecost *pentecoste* (πεντηκοστη) in Greek.
2. The festival of the harvest" or the festival of the harvest of wheat is ***hag ha katzir*** (גח יצקהר) in Hebrew. *Hag* here means the festival, *ha* the article, and *katzir* the harvest. The first fruits of early summer is wheat.

called the "day of the first fruits" (Numbers 28:26).[3] However, the best known name for Pentecost by the Israelites is the Festival of Weeks. The Festival of Weeks means that Pentecost comes after seven weeks. In Hebrew it is the Festival of Weeks.[4] The Israelites call the Festival of Weeks **Shavuot**.

The Israelites kept the Pentecost as an honorable and joyful festival. Following are various reasons for this: first, they were glad to harvest the wheat; second, the harvest of wheat was the First Fruits of early summer; and they had received the Ten Commandments on that day. Naturally, the day was regarded as an honorable day, for they remembered that they had received the Ten Commandments and the Torah through Moses on that day.[5] Additionally, as time progressed, it is also believed that King David, who the Israelites most honored, was born and died on that day.[6]

Biblical Background

Reading the text is significant in order to know the biblical background of this important day of Pentecost, the festival of early summer. Needless to say, this Word was given to the Israelites through Moses as follows:

> From the day after the Sabbath, the day you brought the sheaf of the wave offering, count off seven full weeks. Count off **fifty days** up to the day after the seventh Sabbath, and then present an offering of new grain to the Lord. From wherever you live, bring two loaves made of two-tenths of an ephah of fine flour, baked with yeast, as a wave offering of First Fruits to the Lord. Present with this bread seven male lambs, each a year old and without defect, one young bull and two rams. They will be a burnt offering to the Lord, together with their grain offerings and drink offerings—an offering made by fire, an aroma pleasing to the Lord. Then sacrifice one male goat for a sin offering and two lambs, each a year old, for a fellowship offering. The priest is to wave the two lambs

---

3. It is called **hag ha bikkurim** (גח םירוכבה) in Hebrew, and *bikkurim* here means the first fruits.

4. It is called **hag ha shavuot** (גח תועובשה) in Hebrew, and *shavuot* means weeks.

5. Epstein, *All about Jewish Holidays and Customs*, 68.

6. Ibid., 71.

before the Lord as a wave offering, together with the bread of the First Fruits. They are a sacred offering to the Lord for the priest. On that same day you are to proclaim a sacred assembly and do no regular work. This is to be a lasting ordinance for the generations to come, wherever you live (Leviticus 23:15-21).

As mentioned above, the Pentecost is simultaneously one of the seven festivals of Israel and one of the three major festivals. All men of Israel were required to come to the temple during the three festival seasons—Passover (or the Festival of Unleavened Bread), Pentecost, and the Festival of Tabernacles—and to strictly keep the festivals (Exodus 23:14-17; 32:22; Deuteronomy 16:16; 2 Chronicles 8:13). The Pentecost is the middle of the three festival seasons. In other words, the Pentecost is preceded by Passover and followed by the Festival of Tabernacles.

Like the Sabbath or other festivals, Pentecost is also a holy assembly, therefore no work is allowed. Since the Pentecost is one of the three major festivals, it is included in all of the Pentateuch (the first five books of the Bible) except for Genesis. Of course, since Genesis did not deal with the Law of Moses, the festivals were not formed and therefore never mentioned. The places that the Pentecost is mentioned are as follows: Exodus 23:14-17, Leviticus 23: 15-21, Numbers 28:26-31, and Deuteronomy 16:9-12.

Offerings that the Israelites presented to God in the Pentecost are as follows: first, they made two leavened breads, which produced two-tenths (about four liters) of an ephah, and presented them to God by wavering them before God. They presented these breads as their daily food, as an expression of their thankful minds, to God who blessed them with the daily food.[7] Although the Israelites planted the wheat, cultivated, and harvested it, they knew God ultimately allowed them to have the bread, so they were thankful for His blessing. God had furnished the rain and sunlight and was the Creator of its origin.[8]

---

7. Noordtzij, *Bible Student's Commentary: Leviticus*, 236.

8. Gaster, *A Modern Interpretation and Guide: Festivals of the Jewish Year*, 60.

However, since the two loaves included leaven, they could not place them on the altar of the burnt offering (Cf. Leviticus 2:11). So, which offerings were the Israelites allowed to present? They offered seven-year old lambs without blemish, one young bull, and two rams that were all burned by fire. In addition to these burnt offerings, they offered one male goat for the sin offering, and finally, they offered two one-year old lambs as the sacrificial offering of peace.

Notable here is the presentation of the peace offering after the sin offering. The reason for its importance is simple! The problem of sin had to be solved before real peace could be enjoyed. AT Pentecost, the Israelites could truly have peace only after cleansing their double problem of sin—sin to God and sin to humans. Peace held a double meaning, which included the peace with God above and the peace with humans below.[9]

An important teaching that should not be overlooked regarding the Pentecost is the fact that not only the Israelites would have God's blessing. For this reason, Deuteronomy adds this commandment:

> You and your son and your daughter, your manservant and your maidservant, the Levite who is within your towns, the sojourner, the fatherless, and the widow who are among you, at the place which the Lord your God will choose, to make his name dwell there (Deuteronomy 16:11).

What should be carefully observed from this commandment is the fact that in this joyful fourfold festival—the harvest of wheat, the First Fruits of early summer, the bestowment of the Torah, and the birth of David---regardless of young and old, all should equally have God's blessing. A slave or a Levite, a sojourner or the fatherless and a widow, all have equal status with **you and your children** (the Israelites). This was possible because God was their Creator and Redeemer. For this reason, the Israelites had to enjoy and share with the needy.

Mishnah describes well this picture of enjoying life together and sharing of offerings. Imagine the picture as we read the following:

---

9. Francis, *Celebrate the Festivals of the Lord*, 56.

How were the first-fruits brought up? The populace that lives in the vicinity of the Assembly Head...gathers together in his home town, and everyone sleeps the night in the town's streets. They do not enter into the houses (to circumvent becoming exposed to ritual impurity). Waking them in the morning, the overseer would cry out, "Get up, and let us go up to Zion, to the House of the Lord our God!"

Those who were closest in the procession (to Jerusalem) would carry fresh dates and grapes... Those at the back would carry dried fruits and raisins. An ox is led before them (designated as the offering to accompany the first-fruits) whose horns are overlaid with gold, with an olive branch crown on its head...

A flute was played at the head of the procession, whose sound could be heard from a great distance. Finally they reached the Temple Mount. Upon arriving at the Temple, (the procession) entered inside. Once in the outer court, the Levites would sing: "I will praise you, God, for You have lifted me up, and have not allowed my enemies to rejoice over me" (Psalms 30:1).[10]

Turn of History

Did the astonishingly joyful Pentecost continue incessantly? Of course not! As already mentioned, an event that changed thoroughly the history and way of life of the Israelites occurred. It was the event of an enormous tragedy that occurred in A.D. 70. Even before the event, few Jews were present to welcome the cruel domination of Rome. In A.D. 66, the Jewish people retook Jerusalem and expelled the Roman people.

Rome needed to notify the world of the rigorous consequences of rebellion. Rome sent General Titus who led a strong army, and in the end, Jerusalem was completely destroyed in A.D. 70. At that time, starvation was so severe that even women ate their children.[11] The army of Rome took 97,000 prisoners and relentlessly killed 1,100,000.[12] Because this occurred at the very moment of the Fes-

---

10. Ibid, 57.

11. Flavius Josephus, *The Works of Flavius Josephus: Antiquities of the Jews: A History of the Jewish Wars*, tr. William Whiston (Philadelphia, PA: David McKay Publisher, n. d.), 842-43.

tival of Unleavened Bread, many people had gathered, so the number of victims was greater than it would have normally been at another time.[13]

The Israelites, nevertheless, did not stand back. After gathering power, they attacked with an enormous rebellion again. This event occurred in A.D. 132, when the Emperor of Rome Hadrian reigned. The Israelites succeeded in retaking Jerusalem and expelling the Roman soldiers. Their fighting spirit seemed to reach the sky. The Israelites believed that the golden age of Israel had finally come under the Messiah who was foretold in the Old Testament.[14]

However, before long it was proved that the golden age of Israel had not yet come. Rome sent 35,000 elite soldiers. Although the war lasted for three years, the result was as expected. The Roman elite troops retook Jerusalem in A.D. 135. Not only did they recapture Jerusalem but they also demolished the entire nation of Israel. As a result, 985 towns were devastated, and about fifty cathedrals were destroyed. About 580,000 Jews were killed. Furthermore, countless people died from starvation and diseases. Those who were sold into slavery were countless.[15]

After that time, the Jewish people were not allowed to enter Jerusalem. Whoever entered was killed at the place where he or she stood by summary execution.[16] The Roman soldiers rebuilt Jerusalem in the name of Hadrian, which changed the city to become the city that worshipped the Roman Emperor. Also, they built a temple dedicated to Jupiter on the location of the original temple on Mount Zion. The whole of Jerusalem was downgraded into a playground where the Roman soldiers celebrated their victories.[17]

---

12. Ibid., 855.
13. John SungChul Hong, *Hyeondaineul Wihan BokeumJeondoui SeongKeyongjeok Model* (*Biblical Model of Evangelism for Modern People*), 190-91.
14. Howard & Rosenthal, *The Festivals of the Lord*, 93.
15. Ibid., 94.
16. Later on, in the fourth century, Constantine I allowed them to enter Jerusalem,to repent and pray toward the Western wall, per year, that is, in Abib 9. "The Western Wall," in Wikipedia.
17. Howard & Rosenthal, *The Festivals of the Lord*, 93.

The hope of the Israelites--the hope of independence from Rome and the rebuilding of the temple--came to nothing. The land was so entirely devastated that they could not even farm. Even if they could bring the products from farming to God, they had no temple or altar for burnt offerings. Without the temple, no method was available in order to keep the festivals in accordance with the Law of Moses.

Therefore, since they were required to keep the Law of Moses, the Israelites searched for an alternative. In A.D. 140, the Sanhedrin in the town of Usha near Haifa was convened. They decided to keep the festival in a different way, by commemorating Pentecost as the day of the Torah because they had received the Torah on Mount Sinai during the Pentecost (Exodus 19:1), instead of keeping **Shavuot** (the previous type of Pentecost by offering the agricultural products). This welcomed decision quickly spread among the Israelites.[18]

Festival of Synagogue

In this way, the Israelites came to keep the Pentecost in the synagogue, not in the temple. They read the writings about Pentecost,[19] but the main topic was about the bestowment of the Law. For this reason, they learned the lesson from Exodus 19-20, which deals with the declaration of the Ten Commandments. They recited a poem, which poetically describes Exodus 19 as follows:[20]

> Loud rang the voice of God, and lighting spears
> Pierced all the heavens; thunder shook the spheres,
> And flames leaped forth; and all the angels blew
> Their trumpets, and the earth was riven through.
> Then all the peoples writhed, aghast and pale,
> Like as a woman in her birth-travail

---

18. The Israelites believed that they received the Torah on March 6, the fiftieth day after Passover and crossing the Led Sea. Hartley, *Leviticus*, 386.

19. The articles read at that time were Numbers 28:26-31 and Deuteronomy 15:19-16:17.

20. Gaster, *A Modern Interpretation and Guide: Festivals of the Jewish Year*, 64.

> ...
> To little Sinai bent the skies and came,
> And crowned it with His mist and cloud; and flame
> Of angels wreathed it. Then, amid the sound
> Of thunder, under them that clustered round
> Its foot gave forth His mighty voice; and they
> Replied: O Lord, we hear and will obey.
> And when that they stood waiting, came the word,
> That word that slits the rocks: **I am the Lord**.

The Israelites did not read only this piece. They also rhythmically recited 613 commandments contained in the Pentateuch. Then they read the first chapter of Ezekiel, of which the background was during the period of the exile to Babylon. The first chapter introduces that the same God, who delivered them from Egypt and gave them the Ten Commandments, appeared in the flame and glory on Mount Sinai in order to give the same grace to the captives. To read the core verses in the first chapter of Ezekiel is as follows:

> As I looked, behold, a stormy wind came out of the north, and a great cloud, with brightness round about it, and fire flashing forth continually, and in the midst of the fire, as it were gleaming bronze... Then the Spirit lifted me up, and as the glory of the Lord arose from its place, I heard behind me the sound of a great earthquake (Ezekiel 1:4, 3:12).

After this, they read Habakkuk because the prophet Habakkuk was sure that the same God, who delivered their forefathers from Egypt, would also deliver him and his people who were suffering as the captives of Assyria:

> You came out to deliver your people... You trampled the sea with your horses, churning the great waters. I heard and my heart pounded, my lips quivered at the sound;... yet I will rejoice in the Lord, I will be joyful in God my savior (Habakkuk 3:13, 15-16, 18).

The Israelites then read Psalms 68, a praise song of Pentecost. Its content was also deployed in the same context. This Psalm was the praise song for God Who showered many blessings with His might, after He had brought their forefathers from Egypt. God would do the same for them: When you went out before your people, O God, when you marched through the wasteland, the earth shook,...before God, the One of Sinai, before God, the God of Israel. You gave abundant showers, O God;... Your people settled in it.... (Psalms 68:7-10).

At last, the Israelites read Ruth, for several reasons. First, the book records the fact that Ruth became the grandmother of David (Ruth 4:21-22). As mentioned above, the Israelites commemorated together the birth and death of David in the Pentecost. Second, when starved, Ruth came back to Bethlehem on the harvest of barley day. Although the Pentecost was related to the wheat harvest, Ruth solved hunger with God's grace. Third, it was for them to commemorate the faith of Ruth, who chose the law, in the Pentecost that observes the bestowment of the law.[21]

Since the Pentecost is a special festival, their food was also special. They mainly ate cake made of milk and cheese, because their forefathers received a law on Mount Sinai, which tasted as sweet as milk and honey. They also prayed the following while eating triangular shaped dumplings: "Blessed be the Merciful One who gave the threefold law [Law, Prophets, and Writings] to a people made of three classes [priests, Levites, and Israelites] through a third-born child [Moses was born after Miriam and Aaron]."[22]

In addition to all of this, the Israelites baked two white loaves, called *halla,* to eat on the Sabbath of the Pentecost. The two loaves that they presented to God by wavering in the temple (Leviticus 23:17), symbolized the two stone tablets that Moses had directly received from God. Needless to say, the Ten Commandments were recorded on these stone tablets. As a result, from the beginning of the Pentecost to the end, the Israelites commemorated their gift from God of the Torah.[23]

Fulfillment of the Festival of Pentecost

On the day of Pentecost, one of the three festival seasons of Israel, men of Israel had to come to the temple in Jerusalem and observe the festival. For this reason, Jerusalem was full of the Jewish peo-

---

21. Ibid., 70.
22. Howard & Rosenthal, *The Festivals of the Lord*, 96-97.
23. Ibid., 97.

ple who came from all places. They came from east, west, north, and south like masses of clouds (Acts 2:9-11). When they offered the service of Pentecost in the temple, they read the writing about God Who came in a flame of fire, from Ezekiel 1.

During one Pentecost the Jewish people suddenly met a strange group. The group seemed to have specially met God, as Moses met God. They spoke in different languages in such a way they could understand them. Some Jews misunderstood that they had gotten drunk in the daylight (Acts 2:13). Some Jews began to mock them. As a response to this, the twelve disciples including Peter began to tell them of the Holy Spirit Who had come down to dwelled in them.

On that day, 3,000 people repented and accepted Jesus Christ as their Savior (Acts 2:41). These 3,000 people were the First Fruits of the Holy Spirit, similar to the Israelites' offering of the First Fruits of barley to God. These 3,000 people were just the First Fruits of the enormous harvest that would follow in the future. A few days later, 5,000 people accepted Jesus Christ as their Savior (Acts 4:4). Since then, the fruits of the Holy Spirit have ceaselessly expanded.

Jesus Christ died on the cross as the Paschal lamb and was locked in a tomb (the bread of the Festival of Unleavened Bread), but God raised Him as the First Fruits of resurrection. On the fiftieth day after resurrection--the Pentecost-- Jesus Christ received the Holy Spirit from God and poured down the Spirit to the disciples (Acts 2:33). As the Lord promised, the disciples received *the promise of my Father*, and got the power of the Holy Spirit (Luke 24:49; Acts 1:8). The Holy Spirit did many works through these disciples. Let us study some illustrations of these works.

It was the Holy Spirit that rebuked sinners and led them to repent and believe for their regeneration (John 16:8-11; Acts 2:37-38). That was not all! It was the Holy Spirit sealed these believers (Ephesians 1:13). The purpose of sealing was to prove that ownership was switched from Satan to God. The Holy Spirit also taught the Word of truth to those who are born again (John 16:13).

Furthermore, these Christians were filled with the Holy Spirit so that they were able to overcome their sinful nature and corruption

(Acts 4:31; Ephesians 5:18).[24] Then, the Holy Spirit began to guide them step by step so that they were able to live in righteousness, peace, joy, and glory eventually (2 Corinthians 3:16-17). As Paul said, they are sons of God: *For all who are led by the Spirit of God are sons of God* (Romans 8:14).

The last glorious work of the Holy Spirit for Christians is the work of resurrection. When the Lord comes again, the Holy Spirit will transform all real Christians to be like Christ (1 John 3:2). Paul explains thus: *If the Spirit of him who raised Jesus from the dead dwells in you, he who raised Christ Jesus from the dead will give life to your mortal bodies also through his Spirit which dwells in you* (Romans 8:11).[25]

To sum up these works, the Holy Spirit is the Spirit of Life. The Holy Spirit, who dwelled in those at the Pentecost, brought the spiritually dead to life. In order to accomplish the covenant of God's law in the life of Christians, the Holy Spirit enters their hearts and lives. The Ten Commandments that were given to the Israelites at the Pentecost of the past were not capable of granting eternal life. One proof of it was 3,000 people who got killed because of Ten Commandments (Exodus 32:28). In contrast, on the Pentecost of the New Testament, 3,000 people began to taste eternal life. Paul stated the same thing: *The written code kills, but the Spirit gives life* (2 Corinthians 3:6).

The presence of the Holy Spirit was the fulfillment of Jeremiah's prophecy. It was the Holy Spirit that enabled Christians to keep the Ten Commandments and the Law, which the Israelites could not through their own efforts. Let us quote Jeremiah's prophecy: *But this is the covenant which I will make with the house of Israel after those days, says the LORD: I will put my law within them, and I will write it upon their hearts; and I will be their God, and they shall be my people* (Jeremiah 31:33).

---

24. John Wesley said that it is the experience of entire sanctification. John Sungchul Hong, *Bultaneun Jeondoja John Wesley: Gui Saengaewa Sayuk* (*John Wesley, the Fiery Evangelist*), 7th ed. (Seoul: Saebok Publishing House, 2009), 195 ff.

25. Gustagson deals with the work of the Holy Spirit, succinctly but comprehensively. Roy W. Gustagson, *Festivaling on the Festivals* (Findlay, OH: Dunham Publishing Co., 1958), 58 ff.

Ezekiel was the prophet who specified the covenant of Jeremiah in a clearer way: Listen to his prophecy:

> A new heart I will give you, and a new spirit I will put within you; and I will take out of your flesh the heart of stone and give you a heart of flesh. And I will put my spirit within you, and cause you to walk in my statutes and be careful to observe my ordinances... you shall be my people, and I will be your God (Ezekiel 36:26-28).

The coming of the Holy Spirit upon the disciples on the day of Pentecost is the second most important even next to Jesus' death and resurrection in Christianity. As there were three different kinds of phenomena on the day of Pentecost, so were similar kinds of phenomena when God came down to the Israelites at Mt. Sinai. Moses described the event as follows:

> Now when all the people perceived the thunderings and the lightnings and the sound of the trumpet and the mountain smoking, the people were afraid and trembled; and they stood afar off, and said to Moses, You speak to us, and we will hear; but let not God speak to us, lest we die. And Moses said to the people, Do not fear; for God has come to prove you, and that the fear of him may be before your eyes, that you may not sin (Exodus 20:18-20).

Just as God came in thunder, sounds, and lightning, the Holy Spirit came down in a similar way:

> And suddenly a sound came from heaven like the rush of a mighty wind, and it filled all the house where they were sitting. And there appeared to them tongues as of fire, distributed and resting on each one of them. And they were all filled with the Holy Spirit and began to speak in other tongues, as the Spirit gave them utterance (Acts 2:2-4).

The phenomena when the Holy Spirit came down were: purifying and impassioning fire and powerful wind which was invisible but perceptible.[26]

---

26. Stott summarized into sound, sight and speech the common works that occurred in Mount Sinai and in the festival of Pentecost. John Stott, *The Spirit, the Church and the World: The Message of Acts* (Downers Grove, IL: InterVarsity Press, 1990), 62.

Notable here is the fact that all people who were filled with the Holy Spirit began to speak in different languages. Why did they speak in different languages? The purpose was for powerful evangelism. Yes! The coming of the Holy Spirit was the gift that God gave his people so they could serve others. For this purpose, God commanded the disciples to taste the power of the Holy Spirit and witness from Jerusalem to the ends of the world (Acts 1:8).

The ends of the earth indicate the Gentiles. To our amazement, one offering in Pentecost implied Gentiles, as described in Leviticus 23. It was the two loaves made with leaven to wave before God. One loaf signified Jews and the other the Gentiles.[27] Leaven may indicate imperfect human beings. Although human beings—Jews or Gentiles—are imperfect and sinful, they can be led to regeneration through the redemptive work of Jesus Christ.

Jesus Christ commanded His disciples not to leave Jerusalem and to wait until they experienced the fullness of the Holy Spirit (Acts 1:4). Why did they have to experience the fullness of the Holy Spirit? Jesus Christ clearly said two purposes. One was to spread the gospel to all people (Mark 16:15). The other was for making people of all nations disciples (Matthew 28:19-20).[28] When all born-again and Spirit-filled Christians faithfully carry out this Great Commission of the Lord, the Lord will come again soon. Then and only then, the purpose of the Pentecost will be completed.

---

27. Booker, *Celebrating Jesus in the Biblical Festivals*, 104.

28. In order to study the Great Commission that the Lord repeatedly mentioned toHis disciples five times, see the book, John Sungchul Hong, *Junimeu Jisang Myeongryeong: Seonggyeong Uimiwa Jeokyong* (*The Great Commission of the Lord: Biblical Meaning and Application*).

Chapter 9

The Trumpets

We have studied four festivals thus far, which fell into divisions of festivals of spring and early summer. The festivals of spring—Passover, the Festival of Unleavened Bread and the Festival of First Fruits—were all related to the redemptive event of Jesus Christ. After many days Pentecost arrived. Then, after the dispensation of God the Father and God the Son Jesus, on the day of Pentecost arrived the dispensation of the Holy Spirit. Descent of God's Spirit on earth at Pentecost opened up the new era of the Holy Spirit.

The descent of the Holy Spirit brought about the birth of the Church, and so this era is also called the Church era. Also, since the Gentiles have been playing a main role in this era of the Church, the era is also referred to as the gentile era. Since it was absolutely impossible without God's grace for gentiles to experience salvation and become the center of the Church, it is also called the era of grace (Ephesians 2:8). This era of the Holy Spirit will continue until the Lord which is related to His second coming, is also called the last days (Acts 2:17).

It would be fairly long period of time after the festival of early summer, Pentecost, before the next festivals arrive. These festivals are named the festivals of fall. While the three festivals of spring occur in January, the three festivals of fall occur in July. While the three festivals of spring illuminate the death and resurrection of Jesus Christ, the three festivals of fall illuminate the Second Advent of Christ. Therefore, the three festivals of fall are closely related to the eschatology of Christianity.

In summary, while the three festivals of spring are kept around the event of the cross that took place in the past in Christianity, the three festivals of fall are practiced around the Second Advent in the future. In the middle of these festivals, the Pentecost plays the role of connector between the past and the present, and this connecting role is also the very work of the Holy Spirit and the Church.

The Bible Teaches

In order to learn about the Festival of Trumpets, the first festival of the festivals of fall, let us read its text first of all:

> The Lord said to Moses, Say to the Israelites: On the **first day** of the seventh month you are to have a day of rest, a sacred assembly commemorated **with trumpet blasts**. Do no regular work, but present an offering made to the Lord by fire (Leviticus 23:23-25).

According to this text, it just says to "commemorate with trumpet blasts," without supplying a special name for the event. Although it is named the Festival of Trumpets because of the trumpet blast expression, in fact, it is called "the Head of the New Year" rather than the Festival of Trumpets.[1] The reason is simple! July, according to the sacred calendar of Israel, is the first month of New Year in the civil calendar! Therefore, the Israelites doubly commemorate the Festival of Trumpets. While they commemorate it as the Festival of Trumpets in accordance with the sacred calendar, they also celebrate it as the first day of New Year in accordance with the civil calendar.

Since the Festival of Trumpets is simultaneously the Sabbath and the day of a holy assembly, no work is allowed. In fact, July *Tishr*, as the holiest month in a year for the Jewish people, is the month for them to sincerely come before God, resting for almost a

---

1. The Hebrew name of the Festival of Trumpets is Rosh Hashanaga (שאר הנשה), which means the first day of New Year.

whole month. They commemorate the first day as the Festival of Trumpets, and from then on for ten days they keep as "Days of Awe." And they keep the tenth day as the Day of Atonement. And then they keep the festival of Trumpets from day fifteen to twenty one. The twenty-second day is the last day to finish up all of the festivals.

Not by accident did July become such a noble month. Originally, seven symbolized holy perfection. For this reason, the Israelites kept the Sabbath on the seventh day in the week and the Sabbatical year was every seventh year. When seven years passed seven times, that time became known as the Jubilee. The Pentecost also came seven weeks after the Festival of First Fruits. They kept both the Festival of Unleavened Bread and the Festival of Tabernacles for seven days. As soon as July began, so did the Festival of Tabernacles.

It was God Who through Moses commanded the Israelites to announce the festival by trumpet blasts. When the Israelites spent eleven months on Mount Sinai, God commanded them to make a trumpet that they would blow in due season. In accordance to the sound of the trumpet, they proceeded, convened, went to war, announced festivals and even gave offerings. Let us refer to the Bible regarding this subject:

> The Lord said to Moses: Make two trumpets of hammered silver, and use them for calling the community together and for having the camps set out. When both are sounded, the whole community is to assemble before you at the entrance to the Tent of Meeting. If only one is sounded, the leaders--the heads of the clans of Israel-- are to assemble before you. When a trumpet blast is sounded, the tribes camping on the east are to set out. At the sounding of a second blast, the camps on the south are to set out. The blast will be the signal for setting out. To gather the assembly, blow the trumpets, but not with the same signal. The sons of Aaron, the priests, are to blow the trumpets. This is to be a lasting ordinance for you and the generations to come. When you go into battle in your own land against an enemy who is oppressing you, sound a blast on the trumpets. Then you will be remembered by the Lord your God and rescued from your enemies. Also at your times of rejoicing--your appointed festivals and New Moon festivals--you are to sound the trumpets over your burnt offerings and fellowship offerings, and

they will be a memorial for you before your God. I am the Lord your God (Numbers 10:1-10).

According to this passage, the Israelites blew the trumpet in various cases. For example, they blew to start the seven specially appointed festivals and on the first day of the months. As a result, for the Festival of Trumpets, they blew the trumpet twice. They blew the trumpet not only for the Festival of Trumpets, but also for the first day of the month, since it falls on July 1, which is obviously the first day of the month.

According to the above scripture, God commanded them to make a silver trumpet to blow, as time progressed, it was replaced by a lamb's horn trumpet. This change took place because of the Jubilee. The Jubilee is an important year that comes in the year after the seven Sabbaths of years (forty-nine years), which would be the fiftieth year. In that fiftieth year all slaves were liberated, and all property (which was to lay fallow for two years) reverted to the original owners. On the Day of Atonement of the Jubilee, July 10th, they were required to blow a lamb's horn trumpet: *Then have the trumpet sounded everywhere on the tenth day of the seventh month; on the Day of Atonement sound the trumpet throughout your land. Consecrate the fiftieth year and proclaim liberty...*(Leviticus 25:9-10).[2]

When Abraham tried to offer Isaac as the burnt offering, the horn of a lamb was entangled in the wood and, thus, that lamb was offered as the burnt offering on behalf of Isaac. For the Israelites to come to use the lamb's horn trumpet seems to be rooted in this event. For the Israelites, the lamb's horn became the symbol of "redemption, renewal, and rejoicing."[3] For this reason, on the Day of Atonement or particularly on the Day of Atonement of the Jubilee, they had to blow the lamb's horn trumpet, and this became a tradition. Ever since then, the horn trumpet has been used on important occasions.

---

2. The trumpet here is *shofar* (שופר) in Hebrew, which indicates lamb's horn trumpet.

3. Francis, *Celebrate the Festivals of the Lord*, 68.

For example, when the Israelites received the Torah, the horn trumpet, that is, the *shofar* was used (Exodus 19:19). When Joshua pulled down Jericho, the *shofar* was used, not a silver trumpet (Joshua 6:20). When the lost country of the Israelites was restored, the *shofar* was used again (Isaiah 27:13). When the Israelites are restored with the indwelling of God at the end of the world, the *shofar* will be blown (Zechariah 9:14).

At the Festival of Trumpets, in addition to the burnt offering of the first day of the month, the Israelites presented to God the following: one young bull, one ram, and seven one year old male lambs without blemish as burnt offerings, along with a cereal offering. These offerings became fragrant ones. They also offered one male goat as the sin offering (Numbers 29:1-5).

Tradition Rolls On

The beginning of a new moon was important for the Israelites. They formed a committee to create an observation point from which to observe the event. On seeing the new moon, the committee members ran to Jerusalem and witnessed the following before the Sanhedrin: "We testify that we have seen the new moon." They also reported the exact time that the moon appeared.

The moment was a moment of high excitement for the people. Once the Sanhedrin announced that the new moon had started, responsible persons ran to light fires on the highest hills. As soon as the inhabitants of the closest town saw this signal, they also lit a fire on their highest hill. In this way, continually reaching the farthermost towns, light was shed on the whole country.[4]

At midnight on the eve of the Festival of Trumpets, Jews all over the world went to pray in synagogues. They seriously prayed for repentance and forgiveness. The reason that they prayed such prayers was due to the book of life in heaven. Since all good and evil actions are recorded in the book, the Jews had to receive forgiveness through repentance. They continued to pray the prayers of repentance and forgiveness for ten days.[5]

---

4. Epstein, *All about Jewish Holidays and Customs*, 8.
5. This prayer is called *Selihot*, that is, forgiveness. Ibid., 21-22.

After these prayers, the Jewish people read Psalms 37, which declares that someday God will reign over all peoples. In order to express such a declaration in detail, they blew the horn trumpet, the **shofar**. The meaning of the sound of the trumpet was as follows:

> Awake, ye sleepers, and consider your deeds; remember your Creator and repent. Be not of those who hunt after shadows and who waste their years seeking empty things. Look well into your souls; leave your evil ways and thoughts, and return to God, so that He may have mercy on you.[6]

Of course, they did not blow the horn trumpet recklessly. They had to blow the trumpet according to order and meaning. There were three ways of blowing the trumpet at the Festival of Trumpets. First, they sounded a long blast starting on a low note and raised nearly an octave. Second, they sounded three short and successive blasts. Finally, they sounded nine quick and sharp blasts of a high note. Every man, woman, and child listened to the sound of the trumpet, which symbolized the unity of the people.[7]

After this, they recited another prayer book, and the same also was recited on the Day of Atonement. This prayer book was full of inspiration that produced holiness and awe felt at the Festival of Trumpets.[8] After finishing prayer, they returned to have a meal at home. They shared bread baked in the shape of a ladder, with wine. The ladder expressed their wish that their prayer would go upward to the Almighty in heaven. Then the members of the family said the following greeting of New Year to each other: "O Lord, Grant us a sweet and happy year!"[9]

---

6. Ibid., 23.

7. Ibid. The one long sound implies the sovereignty of God, the three short sounds remembrance, and the nine short and sharp sounds the lamb's horn. Mitch & Zhava

Glaser, *The Fall Festivals of Israel* (Chicago: Moody Press, 1987), 37-38.

8. Epstein, *All about Jewish Holidays and Customs*, 23-24.

9. Ibid, 24.

In the afternoon, the Israelites performed a service for purifying and sin-cleansing. They gathered near a sea or river, or around a well to recite from a prayer book. They were dressed up and recited the prayer book near the water. It was the service of cleansing from their sins. The prayers in the prayer book were composed of Micah 7:18-20, Psalms 118:5-9, Psalms 33, Psalms 130, and Isaiah 11:9. After the prayer, they cast breadcrumbs or dust from their pockets into the water.[10]

The festival of Trumpets was significant in that the beginning of the New Year as well as the forgiveness of past sins through repentance was announced. But that was not all! The people took the Festival of Trumpets as a festival to commemorate the past. What did they commemorate? They commemorated July 1st as the day of God's creation. Remembering God's creation, the Israelites entrusted themselves again to another New Year with God.[11]

In this sense, the Festival of Trumpets was also the festival to reaffirm the covenantal relationship between God and the Israelites. The events that demonstrate well such a covenantal relationship repeatedly occurred on July 1st, and one of them was the relationship between God and Abraham. In accordance with God's commandment, Abraham offered his only son Isaac as a burnt offering. God received Abraham's faith and reaffirmed the covenant they shared. God said: *I will surely bless you and make your descendants as numerous as the stars in the sky and as the sand on the seashore... through your offspring all nations on earth will be blessed, because you have obeyed me* (Genesis 22:17-18). This promise was not given to him because Abraham offered his son, but was given to reaffirm the covenant that God already had with Abraham (Cf. Genesis 12:3; 15:6).

Abraham was not the only person to run into covenantal relationship with God on the first day of New Year. Hanna was another

---

10. This prayer book is *Tashlikh*, which came after the last word of Micah 7:19: "You will cast all our sins into the depths of the sea." Howard & Rosenthal, *The Festivals of the Lord*, 109-10.

11. Gaster, *A Modern Interpretation and Guide: Festivals of the Jewish Year*, 108.

person who gave birth to Samuel on July 1st.[12] Hanna made a covenant with God and that covenant is in her prayer:

> O Lord Almighty, if you will only look upon your servant's misery and remember me, and not forget your servant but give her a son, then I will give him to the Lord for all the days of his life, and no razor will ever be used on his head (1 Samuel 1:11).

God received her covenant and granted Hanna a son. The priest Eli responded on behalf of God: *Go in peace, and may the God of Israel grant you what you have asked of him* (1 Samuel 1:17). In the case of Abraham, God commanded first and then Abraham obeyed; in this manner the covenant was accomplished. By contrast, however in the case of Hanna, she promised first and God accepted; then their covenant was realized.[13]

The prayer of blessing was indispensible in various services of the first day of the New Year. During the day, they prayed the prayer of blessing no less than eighteen times. The prayer was summarized as this: "Remember us for life, O King who delights in life; inscribe us in the Book of Life, for Thy sake, God of life."[14] This prayer included remembrance, the kingship of God, and the idea of judgment. Above all, it included the joy of a new beginning.

---

12. Ibid., 111-12.

13. Additionally, the Israelites remembered the things that happened on July 1: (1) God completed creation by creating Adam and Eve (Genesis 1:27); (2) God banished Adam and Eve from the Garden of Eden (Genesis 3:23); (3) Cain and Abel were born (Genesis 4:1-2), each with a twin sister; (4) Cain killed his brother Abel (Genesis 4:8); (5) Cain and his father, Adam, repented of their respective sins, and God forgave them; (6) In the days of the great Flood, the waters began to recede (Genesis 8:1); (7) Sarah and Rachel conceived, respectively (Genesis 21:2; 25:21); (8) At age 137, Abraham tookhis 37 year old son, Isaac, to be sacrificed on Mount Moriah (Genesis 22:3); (9) Sarah, Abraham's wife, died (Genesis 23:1-2); (10) Rebecca, wife of Isaac, died (Genesis 49:31); and (11) Joseph was freed from Pharaoh's prison (Genesis 41:39-44). Francis, *Celebratethe Festivals of the Lord*, 70.

14. Gaster, *A Modern Interpretation and Guide: Festivals of the Jewish Year*, 115.

Expect Its Fulfillment

As mentioned in the preface, the Festival of Trumpets implies prophecy of the future. The festivals of spring—Passover, the Festival of Unleavened Bread and the Festival of First Fruits—imply the already accomplished prophecy through the redemptive death and resurrection of Jesus Christ. Although the Pentecost was already accomplished through the coming of the Holy Spirit in the past, the prophecy of the Pentecost is also being accomplished through the indwelling and power of the Holy Spirit in the present. In contrast, however, the festivals of fall--the Festival of Trumpets, the Day of Atonement and the Festival of Tabernacles--imply the history of the future.

Of these festivals of fall, the Festival of Trumpets is very distinctive because the festival implies the accomplishment of the past and the future at the same time. How was the Festival of Trumpets accomplished in the past? As mentioned above, the Israelites blew the horn trumpet at the Festival of Trumpets, based on a remembrance of the devout faith of Abraham who offered his son Isaac. Abraham took Isaac to Mount Moriah and *bound his son Isaac and laid him on the altar, on top of the wood. Then he reached out his hand and took the knife to slay his son...* (Genesis 22:9-10).

A word of note here is "**bound.**" In Hebrew, the word is *akedah* (עקדה). In the Festival of trumpets during which each person should examine oneself thoroughly, the Israelites asked God for forgiveness through repentance, sometimes depending on the exploits of Abraham, their forefather. Although they did not depend on only Abraham, he was a major representative figure. They did request God grant them mercy, remembering his exploits. Let us study their prayer:

> Remember unto us, O Lord our God, the covenant and the lovingkindness and the oath which Thou swore unto Abraham our father on Mount Moriah: and consider the binding with which he suppressed his compassion in order to perform thy will with a perfect heart. So may Thy compassion overbear Thine anger against us; in

Thy great goodness may Thy great wrath turn aside from Thy people, Thy city, and Thine inheritance.[15]

The binding of Isaac, that is, **akedah** was deeply latent in the thought of the Jewish people. The binding of Isaac whom the Israelites deeply depended on in the Festival of Trumpets was a good model for Jesus Christ. Isaac and Jesus had surprising commonalities in the following ways. First, the births of Isaac and Jesus were impossible without the interception of God. Second, just as Isaac was not taken because of his sin or unrighteousness on Mount Moriah, so Jesus was not taken to Mount Calvary because of his sin or unrighteousness. Third, at his young age, Isaac absolutely obeyed the commandment of his old father, which was to give up his life. The obedience of Jesus Christ was also that He gave His life. *Although he was a son, he learned obedience from what he suffered and, once made perfect...* (Hebrews 5:8-9). Fourth, figuratively speaking, it can be said that Isaac died and lived again (Hebrews 11:19). Needless to say, Jesus Christ died on the cross and arose. This kind of perfect typology was not easy found![16]

How is the Festival of Trumpets related to the future of Christianity? The Festival of Trumpets is deeply related to creation as well as recreation. Trumpet closely has to do with the descent of God. When He came down to the exodus people, the Israelites, God came with great trumpet blast. *The Lord descended on it in fire... The sound of the trumpet grew louder and louder... The Lord descended to the top of Mount Sinai...* (Exodus 19:18-20).

Also, when the same God comes again from heaven to earth, He will come with wind, the fire of glory, and the sound of the trumpet. The prophet Zechariah who prophesized the Second Coming of Yahweh God said: Then the Lord will appear over them; his arrow will flash like lightning. The Sovereign Lord will sound the trumpet; he will march in the storms of *the south* (Zechariah 9:14). This

---

15. Glaser, *The Fall Festivals of Israel*, 66.
16. Besides these four, more similarities exist. Kevin Williams, The Holidays of God: Fall Festivals (Grand Rapids, MI: RBC Ministries, 2004), 11.

description of the Second Advent of the Messiah may be enough to remind us of the Descent of God onto Mount Sinai.

The Second Advent of the Messiah foretold for the Israelites was also for the Church. The reason is simple! The Church has become an eschatological community with the presence of the Holy Spirit. It is because the Holy Spirit indwells in individual Christians who make up the community. When the Messiah Jesus Christ comes again with the trumpet blast, it is biblical that all believers of the true Church will be radically transformed.

The Apostle Paul declared such a transformation as follows: *Listen, I tell you a mystery: We will not all sleep, but we will all be changed—in a flash, in the twinkling of an eye, at the last trumpet. For the trumpet will sound, the dead will be raised imperishable, and we will be changed* (1 Corinthians 15:51-52). This word is enough to remind us of the Festival of Trumpets in the Old Testament. When the Lord comes again, the dead and the living Christians up to that point will be changed in the twinkling of an eye.

How will they be changed? The following verse answers: *For the perishable must clothe itself with the imperishable, and the mortal with immortality* (1 Corinthians 15:53). Then each **born again Christian** will be changed to the eternal body to be with the Lord forever. The Apostle John described such a change in this way: *...When he appears, we shall be like him, for we shall see him as he is* (1 John 3:2).

When **born again Christians are changed**, they will be brought up into the air with the Holy Spirit. This is called the rapture. Read the Apostle Paul's prophecy:

> Brothers, we do not want you to be ignorant about those who fall asleep, or to grieve like the rest of men, who have no hope. We believe that Jesus died and rose again and so we believe that God will bring with Jesus those who have fallen asleep in him. According to the Lord's own word, we tell you that we who are still alive, who are left till the coming of the Lord, will certainly not precede those who have fallen asleep. For the Lord himself will come down from heaven, with a loud command, with the voice of the archangel and with the trumpet call of God, and the dead in Christ will rise first. After that, we who are still alive and are left will be caught up together with them in the clouds to meet the Lord in the

air. And so we will be with the Lord forever (1 Thessalonians 4:13-17).

After Christians are brought up, the Holy Spirit and the true Church will no longer be on earth. The world without the Holy Spirit and the Church which held back "the secret power of lawlessness" will be in tremendous chaos and distress (2Thessalonica 2:7). Jesus Christ called this chaos the great tribulation (Matthew 24:21). We will study this tribulation in detail in the next chapter. In a word, the terrible situation of the tribulation will defy any description.[17]

Then, how will **born again Christians** be raptured? According to the Word of God, they will be changed into beautiful brides if they pass three tests. First, they should pass the judgment of fire. Of course, this is not judgment to determine eternity. The judgment was already resolved when they accepted Jesus Christ as the Savior before rapture. The judgment of fire that they must pass through will be about their exploits.

Let us read the teaching of the Apostle Paul:

> If any man builds on this foundation using gold, silver, costly stones, wood, hay or straw, his work will be shown for what it is, because the Day will bring it to light. It will be revealed with fire, and the fire will test the quality of each man's work. If what he has built survives, he will receive his reward. If it is burned up, he will suffer loss; he himself will be saved, but only as one escaping through the flames (1 Corinthians 3:12-15).

Only gold, silver and jewels can pass the judgment of fire, because they passed fire on earth. They are invaluable, though small in size. By contrast, however, wood, grass and straw are large only in volume but small in value, and cannot stand fire.. These kinds of Christians will manage to be saved, but not receive the reward. In contrast, under any circumstance and condition in the world, Christians who maintained the life of holiness and sanctification, remaining chaste and clean, will receive great reward.

The second test that Christians should pass at the time of rapture is their deeds in the world. Let us read the teaching of Paul: *For we*

---

17. This is called seven year great distress.

must all appear before the judgment seat of Christ, that each one may receive what is due him for the things done while in the body, whether good or bad (2 Corinthians 5:10). Before the Lord watching every deed of Christians with His eyes like blazing fire, all will appear and be judged (Revelation 1:14). However, this judgment is not about salvation, but about what they did after their salvation.

The third test that Christians should pass at the time of rapture is to directly report to God about their own life. Let us again read the Apostle Paul's teaching: *So then, each of us will give an account of himself to God* (Romans 14:12). Whatever Christians secretly think or whatever they say and do, they are known to two persons, Jesus Christ and themselves. However painful the process may be, all will have to report their word and deed before God.

As Christians have gone through these three fiery tests and have been purified and sanctified, they will become the bride to the groom (Ephesians 5:26-27). Jesus Christ who was crucified for their purification will become their bride. The long awaited wedding will be inaugurated. The groom Jesus Christ will inaugurate the wedding with a bride who is cleanly dressed in linen (Revelation 19:6-8). To put this fact into diagram is as follows:

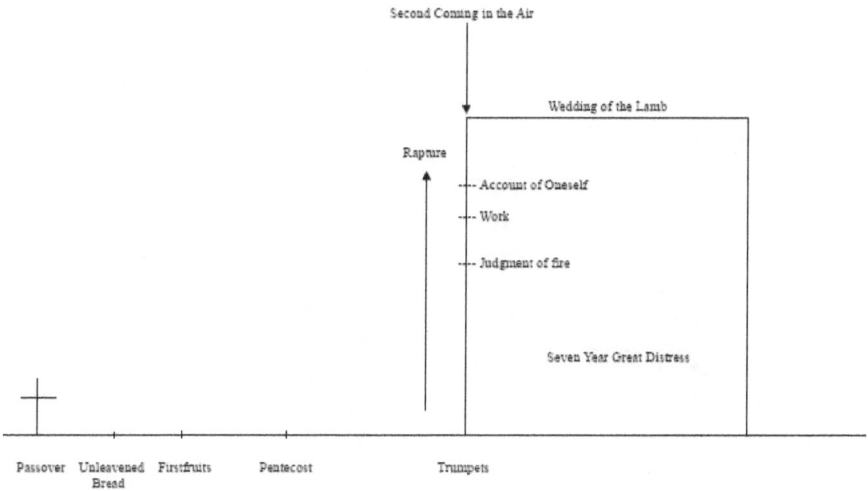

Chapter 10

The Day of Atonement

The Day of Atonement was set by the Word of God. We can explore some facts based on the Word described in Leviticus 23 and on other traditions. First of all, let us review Leviticus 23 in order to further illustrate the facts:

> The Lord said to Moses, The tenth day of this seventh month is the Day of Atonement. Hold a sacred assembly and deny yourselves, and present an offering made to the Lord by fire. Do no work on that day, because it is the Day of Atonement, when atonement is made for you before the Lord your God. Anyone who does not deny himself on that day must be cut off from his people. I will destroy from among his people anyone who does any work on that day. You shall do no work at all. This is to be a lasting ordinance for the generations to come, wherever you live. It is a Sabbath of rest for you, and you must deny yourselves. From the evening of the ninth day of the month until the following evening you are to observe your Sabbath (Leviticus 23:26-32).

The Day of Atonement is *Tishr*, July 10, is the day to finish one's repentance that starts during the Festival of Trumpets. The Day of Atonement in the literal sense of the word is the day to solve the problem of sin. In Hebrew, it means the day to cover sin. To cover in Hebrew is ***kaphar***, which is called **Yom Kippur** in

English.[1] The Day is the day for the Israelites to be liberated from all sins done for the previous year. Their problem of sin ias to be covered on the Day of Atonement, once per year.

The Day of Atonement used to resolve the problem of sin was regarded as the holiest festival of the seven festivals of the Jewish people. For this reason, the Israelites had a time of repentance and prayer no less than ten days from the beginning of Festival of Trumpets. Of course, although the One who forgave their sins on the Day of Atonement was God, human beings were to thoroughly prepare for it. First, they should be ready to receive forgiveness. Second, the high priest was required to prepare well. If he was not prepared, all performances of the day were nullified. Third, they were to prepare offerings because they received forgiveness from God through proper offerings.

First, what did **the Israelites** prepare? They were to "**deny**" themselves, which means fasting (Leviticus 23:29, 32).[2] They had to fast and repent of their sins of the past year. Whoever did not do so was cut off from their people (Leviticus 23:29). In other words, those people were no longer regarded as Israelites. Also, they were not to do any work. Anyone who violated the law was also killed (Leviticus 23:30).

Then, **the high priest** was also required to prepare thoroughly. If he did not prepare himself thoroughly and properly, the service of the day was invalidated, causing the Israelites to have to wait for one more year. The reason was simple! He was to present himself before the most holy God. If the high priest came before God unprepared, he would be killed, and the Israelites had no day of repentance.

Although the high priest would wear a resplendent priest robe, his apparent preparation itself was not good enough. The mediation between God and the Israelites was so important that he was required to a full preparation. His preparation began seven days before the Day of Atonement by remain religiously pure by all means.

---

1. The Day of Atonement is ***Yom Kippurim*** (יום הכיפורים) in Hebrew.

2. This is the only biblical saying that includes not only the commandment of fasting, but repentance, which was later added to this word (Zechariah 7:2-5, 8:19). Noordtzij, *Bible Student's Commentary: Leviticus*, 238.

On that day in particular, he had to purify himself by dipping his body into the water five times. Furthermore, from that day on around five hundred Levites closely surrounded him so that he would not be contaminated.[3]

The high priest came out of his house seven days before the Day of Atonement. He had to stay in a room in the temple, in order to keep him from being contaminated in his house. Although he was so thoroughly careful against contamination, two times a day he washed his body with water mixed with the ashes of a red male calf. This washing was necessary just in case of him becoming unclean unconsciously by touching a dead body (Numbers 19:9).[4] The approach toward a holy God was that of extreme care.

Last, how were **offerings** prepared? For the preparation of offerings, Numbers 29 had to be read. Just for reference, the preparation of the Israelites was described in Leviticus 23, and that of the high priest was described in Leviticus 16. Offerings were composed of one young bull, one ram, and seven one year old lambs without blemish, with a cereal offering added to each animal. All of these offerings were separate from the sin offering and the daily burnt offering (Numbers 29:8-11).

Entering Inside

Since the Day of Atonement was so important to the Israelites, God let them know in detail about the services of the Day of Atonement through Moses:

> This is how Aaron is to enter the sanctuary area: with a young bull for a sin offering and a ram for a burnt offering. He is to put on the sacred linen tunic, with linen undergarments next to his body; he is to tie the linen sash around him and put on the linen turban. These are sacred garments; so he must bathe himself with water before he puts them on. From the Israelite community he is to take two male goats for a sin offering and a ram for a burnt offering. Aaron is to offer the bull for his own sin offering to make atonement for himself and his household. Then he is to take the two goats and present them before the Lord at the entrance to the Tent of Meet-

---

3. Williams, *The Holidays of God: Fall Festivals*, 13.
4. Williams, *The Holidays of God: Fall Festivals*, 13.

ing. He is to cast lots for the two goats—one lot for the Lord and the other for the scapegoat. Aaron shall bring the goat whose lot falls to the Lord and sacrifice it for a sin offering. But the goat chosen by lot as the scapegoat shall be presented alive before the Lord to be used for making atonement by sending it into the desert as a scapegoat... He is to take a censer full of burning coals from the altar before the Lord and two handfuls of finely ground fragrant incense and take them behind the curtain. He is to put the incense on the fire before the Lord, and the smoke of the incense will conceal the atonement cover above the Testimony, so that he will not die. He is to take some of the bull's blood and with his finger sprinkle it on the front of the atonement cover; then he shall sprinkle some of it with his finger seven times before the atonement cover. He shall then slaughter the goat for the sin offering for the people and take its blood behind the curtain and do with it as he did with the bull's blood: He shall sprinkle it on the atonement cover and in front of it. In this way he will make atonement for the Most Holy Place because of the uncleanness and rebellion of the Israelites, whatever their sins have been. He is to do the same for the Tent of Meeting, which is among them in the midst of their uncleanness... He is to lay both hands on the head of the live goat and confess over it all the wickedness and rebellion of the Israelites—all their sins—and put them on the goat's head. He shall send the goat away into the desert in the care of a man appointed for the task. The goat will carry on itself all their sins to a solitary place; and the man shall release it in the desert (Leviticus 16:3-10, 12-16, 21-22).

On the basis of this text, we can create a scenario as follows. Even if he was the high priest, he could enter the Most Holy Place, the place that God enthrones, only on the Day of Atonement once a year. However, since the high priest was also a sinner before God, he, first of all, should solve the problem of his sin. He had to wash his body with water and wear white linen undergarments. Then he was to kill a bull for the sake of his sin. With a censer in one hand and a bowl of blood in the other hand, he could then enter the Most Holy Place.

At that moment, he put his life on God. Unless God accepted him, he would be instantly killed on the place where he stood. He entered in fear and trembling, placing the censer before himself so that the smoke-screen was made between God and himself. He was so hidden that he could escape death. Then with his finger, he sprinkled the blood seven times on the mercy seat above which God enthrones, and again seven times in front of it. Then he walked out backward from the Most Holy Place.

Usually none of the Israelites could call the name of Yahweh because it was too fearful. However, on that day only, the high priest could call the name of Yahweh ten times. When the priest called, "Yahweh," the Israelites fell on their faces and called out, "Blessed be the Name; the glory of His kingdom is forever and ever."[5] Then, the high priest killed a goat.

The death of the goat was the substitutional death for the sin of the Israelites. The high priest for the blood killed the goal selected by lot.[6] Although it had no sin, the goat died for the Israelites. With its blood, the high priest entered the Most Holy Place again. This time was for the atonement of the sins of the Israelites. Like the first time, he sprinkled the blood on the mercy seat seven times and then before the east of the mercy seat seven times.

The high priest walked out to wash his body and put on the robe of priest. This robe was indescribably beautiful and glorious. A plate of pure gold with engraved "holy to the Lord" was put on the turban. On both shoulders, two onyx stones were placed, and the names of the six tribes of Israel were engraved on one stone and the remaining six on the other. On the breast, the breastplate was placed, which included the gemstones with the engraved names of the twelve tribes. By bearing the names on his shoulders and embracing them on his breast, the high priest dedicated his power and mind to the people.

The ephod under the breastpiece was a beautiful one made of embroidery of gold, blue, purple and scarlet yarn on white linen. The robe under the ephod was blue, which reached from neck to knee, and around the hem of the robe ten gold bells and ten pome-

---

5. Williams, *The Holidays of God: Fall Festivals*, 13.

6. For this lottery, they make a specially designed golden box and put two goldentablets in the box, on which are written "for Yahweh" and "for Azazel." After the high priest shakes the box, he thrusts both hands in and withdraws one tablet in each hand. If the tablet marked "for Yahweh" emerges in his right hand, it is regarded as a favorable sign. The goat bleeds and dies for God. Francis, *Celebrate the Festivals of theLord*, 79.

granates were alternately placed. The sound of the bells rang when the high priest came out of the door of the tabernacle. The sound was a blessed good news, telling the people that God had accepted their redemptive goat.[7]

The high priest, who acted for God, could only be beautiful and glorious. He was to declare that all sins of the Israelites were forgiven in the milieu of God. Prior to this declaration, however, he had to show them that their sins had been completely eradicated. Laying his hands on the head of the goat for Azazel, he confessed all unrighteousness and sins of the Israelites. This ritual served to transfer their sins to the goat.

Then, the high priest let the already appointed person drive the goat into an uninhabited into the wilderness. It was as if the Israelites were watching with their own eyes that their sins were also going away as far as the goat was being driven away. At last, the goat disappeared from their sight completely, and it signified that their unrighteousness and sins were completely gone.[8]

Of course, the two goats were regarded as one offering. Leviticus clearly mentions it: *From the Israelite community he is to take two male goats for a sin offering* (Leviticus 16:5). Here, a sin offering meant one offering: *two male goats for a sin offering*. Simply put, for one sin offering two male goats were killed. In this way, with the assurance of forgiveness, the Israelites went back home.

In Synagogue

Since the historical event of A.D. 70, the Israelites could not inaugurate the Day of Atonement in the temple because there was no

---

7. For the cloth of the priest in detail, refer to Exodus 28 and 39.

8. As time went, this tradition of goat was also changed. With tied with a scarlet thread, the goal for Azazel was driven off a cliff. Someday, this thread is reported to have miraculously turned white, indicating that God had accepted their sacrifice and forgiven the nation of Israel. It was believed that this was in fulfillment of Isaiah 1:18, "Though your sins are like scarlet, they shall be as white as snow; though they are red like crimson, they shall be as wool." Williams, *The Holidays of God: Fall Festivals*, 15.

temple or priest. Therefore, the service of the Day of Atonement, which was so important, could only be endorsed in the synagogue. Then, synagogue held the inauguration of the Day of Atonement, which was the most important festival in Israel. On that day, all things were decorated in white, the color of a humble and wounded mind. A chest containing the Torah scroll and the reader's table were also covered with a white tablecloth. White flowers decorated the synagogue, and the worshipers wore white.[9]

The services of the Day of Atonement started from nine on its eve. Israelites lit a candle to enter a synagogue, and the candle symbolized the light of the law that Moses brought down from Mount Sinai on the Day of Atonement. When they entered the synagogue, they were surrounded with fear and awe, due to the thought of the Day of Atonement on the next day. When all people were holding their breath, elders extracted the Torah scroll from the chest. Repentant worshippers kissed the scroll assuring that they would respect the law in the New Year.[10]

The Day of Atonement started at sunset. Before sunset, the elders put the scroll back into the chest. At that moment, they read a prayer book with the spirit of repentance concerning any oaths that they might break during the coming year. They read the book three times. The first time the reader read it very softly, the second time he read somewhat louder and the third time he read more loudly. To read this prayer book was to express their grief over their sinfulness and their cry for the forgiveness from God.[11]

At last, the holy assembly of the Day of Atonement gathered. The day was not only the holy assembly but also a Sabbath of Sabbaths. From the Word of God we read of its importance: *It is a Sabbath of rest, and you must deny yourselves; it is a lasting ordinance* (Leviticus 16:31). The Israelites could not do "partaking of food, drinking, washing, anointing, wearing shoes, and sexual intercourse." They were required to humbly spend the whole day in

---

9. Howeard & Rosenthal, *The Festivals of the Lord*, 127.
10. Glaser, *The Fall Festivals of Israel*, 114.
11. This prayer book is called *Kol Nidre*—all oaths. Ibid, 114-7.

fasting and praise. Of course, one who was ill or weak was exempted from fasting.[12]

As mentioned above, the Israelites had days of repentance for ten days from the Festival of Trumpets, from July 1st to the Day of Atonement, July 10. On the Day of Atonement, the high priest called the name of Yahweh ten times. Each time he called His name, the Israelites confessed their sins. So they confessed their sins ten times on that day. They also recited the Ten Commandments. Ten might be the number of perfection. Therefore, the Israelites perfectly repented of their sins on the Day of Atonement.[13]

The confession of sins ten times was the most important practice on the Day of Atonement. The leader recited the alphabetical list of sins by twos. For example, in the case of alphabet b, the leader recited, "We have sinned through *b*lindness of judgment and through *b*lasphemy of tongue." In alphabet c, he recited, "We have sinned through carnal *c*oncupiscence and *c*landestinely or *c*learly." In alphabet d, he recited, "We have sinned through *d*esignedly, *d*eliberately and through open *d*eclaration." Each time the sins were named, the Israelites repented, beating their breasts. Although someone did not commit the named sin, he or she repented because he or she was one of the people who could have such a sin.

Every time they repented their sins of a certain category, they ended with this expression: "For all of these, O Thou forgiving God, pardon us, and shrive us, and forgive!"[14] Then, they confessed: "We are Thy people!" These are the expressions of intimate relationship between God and the Israelites. Since they confessed their sins based on this relationship, they pleaded for God to forgive.[15]

In the morning, while reading the Torah, particularly Leviticus 16 and Numbers 29:7-11, they learned of the ways and offerings by which their forefathers were cleansed from sins. They also read Isaiah 57:14-58:14 among the prophetic writings to learn how the

---

12. Gaster, *A Modern Interpretation and Guide: Festivals of the Jewish Year*, 151-52.

13. Glaser, *The Festivals of Israel*, 110.

14. Gaster, *A Modern Interpretation and Guide: Festivals of the Jewish Year*, 154.

15. Glaser, *The Festivals of Israel*, 120.

services of the Day of Atonement were gradually developed into the customs of the Jewish people.[16]

In the afternoon, they read the book of Jonah. The reason they chose this book was that its theme is about repentance. Although Jonah rejected the commandment of God, he surely returned to God through true repentance, and could therefore gain the mercy of God. Likewise, they read the book of Jonah in order to show that although they were serious sinners, or even idol worshipers, if they truly repented and showed the proper fruit of repentance, they could be forgiven.[17]

At sunset, the Israelites offered the closing service. To announce the closing was nothing but the pronouncement of their faith. They pronounced it this way:[18]

> "Hear O Israel, the Lord is our God, the Lord is One." (recited once)
>
> "Blessed be the name of His glorious kingdom forever and ever." (recited three times).
>
> "The Lord, He is God." (recited seven times).

To recite "Hear..." just one time was to remind them of the only God. To recite the second sentence three times was to emphasize the kingship of God over past, present, and future. Lastly, to recite the third expression seven times was because God is perfect. With this recitation, the entire congregation rose, and a trumpet was blown one long time. To respond to this sound, they answered, "Next year in Jerusalem!"

---

16. Gaster, *A Modern Interpretation and Guide: Festivals of the Jewish Year*, 165.

17. Ibid., 170 ff.

18. The closing service is Neilah, which originally means "to close door." Glaser, *The Festivals of Israel*, 123.

Looking back

The Day of Atonement, which is the most important festival for the Israelites, is also important to Christianity because the Day of Atonement is accomplished in Christianity in a twofold way. On the one hand, it was accomplished in the past, and on the other it will also be accomplished in the future. First, we will learn when and how the Day of Atonement was accomplished in the past and then how and through whom the Day of Atonement will be accomplished.

First, in order to see how the Day of Atonement of Judaism was already accomplished, let us look at the key word used in relation to atonement in the Old and New Testament. The word is Mercy Seat. As mentioned above, the high priest entered the Most Holy Place once a year to meet God enthroned above on the Mercy Seat. Remember, in order to meet God, the priest took the blood of an offering to sprinkle on the Mercy Seat seven times. Through the blood, God not only met the high priest, but also forgave the sin of the priest as well as all sins of the Israelites committed in the previous year. The Mercy Seat is a cover to cover the Ark of the Covenant. The Ark of the Covenant contains the Ten Commandments. Unless it is covered, the Israelites, who broke the Ten Commandments and the other laws, could only be judged. One day, when the people of Beth Shemesh opened the cover to look into the Ark of the Covenant, many people were killed as judgment (1 Samuel 6:19).

A cover or a lid translated into the Mercy Seat is *Kaporet* in Hebrew, which is translated as propitiation in the New Testament (Hebrew 9:5).[19] Significantly, this word translated into propitiation was related to Jesus Christ. Let us quote the Word:

> God presented him as a sacrifice of atonement (propitiation), through faith in his blood. He did this to demonstrate his justice, because in his forbearance he had left the sins committed beforehand unpunished... so as to be just and the one who justifies those who have faith in Jesus (Romans 3:25-26).

---

19. *Kaporet* (כפורת) in the Old Testament is *hilasterion* (ἱλαστήριον) in the Greek of the New Testament.

According to this word, Jesus Christ became propitiation by His blood and death. In light of the Day of Atonement of Judaism, Jesus Christ was like the dead goat that took all sins of the Israelites. What is different between the goat and Jesus Christ? He by Himself played the role of two goats—one for Yahweh and the other for Azazel. Moreover, Jesus Christ became propitiation for all believers—Israelites and Gentiles.

On the Day of Atonement of Judaism, no forgiveness of sins was granted without blood (Leviticus 17:11). When the high priest sprinkled the blood on the Mercy Seat seven times, God forgave the sins of the Israelites. Likewise, Jesus' blood shed on the cross, the wrath of God toward sinners was propitiated. In other words, all people who are coming before God depending on His blood are justified, however great their sins may be, and whichever ethnic group they may belong.

That is to say that believers can come before God any time through the sacrificial atonement of Jesus Christ. While only the high priest could come before God only once a year in Judaism, anyone can always come before God in Christianity. As if He proved the fact, when Jesus Christ died on the cross, the curtain between the Most Holy Place and the holy place was tore from top to bottom (Matthew 27:51; Luke 23:45).

The author of Hebrews says that the Day of Atonement was accomplished through Jesus Christ in this way:

> He did not enter by means of the blood of goats and calves; but he entered the Most Holy Place once for all by his own blood, having obtained eternal redemption. The blood of goats and bulls and the ashes of a heifer sprinkled on those who are ceremonially unclean sanctify them so that they are outwardly clean. How much more, then, will the blood of Christ, who through the eternal Spirit offered himself unblemished to God, cleanse our consciences from acts that lead to death, so that we may serve the living God! (Hebrews 9:12-14).

The following diagram shows that the Day of Atonement of Judaism was accomplished through Christ. As this diagram shows, in the court of the tabernacle an animal was killed with its blood poured out and its blood sprinkled on the mercy seat in the most holy place. All these activities were accomplished through Jesus Christ. He was the perfect sacrifice of atonement and perfect mer- cy seat. By His blood, He became propitiation that took on all the sins of human beings (1 John 2:2).

Looking Forward

The Day of Atonement is the biggest festival for the Israelites. They gather in the temple once a year and thoroughly repent of their past sins as well as the sins of the coming year. The merciful God forgives them. At the same time, the Day of Atonement is also the biggest festival for the Church because Jesus Christ accomplished the Day of Atonement. However, the Israelites still do not accept Jesus Christ as the Messiah. Spiritually, they are still in the dark.

When will the Israelites that God so loved be atoned? In other words, when will the Day of Atonement be accomplished for them? The day will come! In the Old Testament, God repeatedly foretold about the great and dreadful day of the Lord and salvation:

> The sun will be turned to darkness and the moon to blood before the coming of the great and dreadful day of the Lord. And everyone who calls on the name of the Lord will be saved… there will be deliverance, as the Lord has said, among the survivors whom the Lord calls. (Joel 2:31-32)

The Israelites, the eldest children of God, will one day be forgiven of their sins. Prior to this national redemption, however, they will have to pass through trials. Let us explore how the Day of Atonement will be accomplished for them step by step. As mentioned in the previous chapter (the Festival of Trumpets), after the Church is raptured up, the world will run into great tribulation. Of course, all the religious people and Jews cannot escape this tribulation because they did not accept Jesus Christ as their Savior.

But, God will increase His mercy and reduce some days of the seven year great tribulation for the elect (Matthew 24:22). If it were not for such mercy, no one could be saved, because the tribulation will be too severe. For then there will be great distress, unequaled from the beginning of the world until now—and never to be equaled again (Matthew 24:21). Then, how are their days of distress reduced? For this, let us turn to Daniel:

> He will confirm a covenant with many for one 'seven.' In the middle of the 'seven' he will put an end to sacrifice and offering. And on a wing he will set up an abomination that causes desolation, un- til the end that is decreed is poured out on him (Daniel 9:27).

Here, one seven designates seven years. So the great distress will last for seven years.

For seven years, many will have a covenant with the anti-Christ. In particular, he has a covenant with Israel and gives false peace religiously, economically, and politically. However, during the half of the seven years --"a time, times and half a time"--later, he breaks the covenant (Daniel 7:25, 12:7; Revelation 12:14). The hardship that will come upon them is ineffable, which is well described in Revelation (Revelation 6-18).

The anti-Christ puts an end to sacrifice and offerings for the Israelites, sets up an abominating animal, puts himself forward, and calls himself God. Let us study the prophecy of the Apostle Paul:

> For until the rebellion occurs and the man of lawlessness is revealed, the man doomed to destruction. He will oppose and will exalt himself over everything that is called God or is worshiped, so that he sets himself up in God's temple, proclaiming himself to be God (2 Thessalonians 2:3-4).

At that time the Israelites, who will depend on the Word of God, will war against the anti-Christ, as their forefathers warred against the great army of Rome. The Word that they will depend on is Zechariah 12. Let us read part of it:

> I am going to make Jerusalem a cup that sends all the surrounding peoples reeling... all the nations of the earth are gathered against her... On that day I will strike every horse with panic...I will keep a watchful eye over the house of Judah... Jerusalem will remain intact in her place (Zechariah 12:2-4, 6).

This war is the famous Armageddon War (Revelation 16:16). The war between the army of Israel that will come in the name of God and the armies of the kings who surround Israel will be extremely brutal. One of the reasons this war will be brutal is that evil spirits lie behind the kings who will gather against Israel (Revelation 16:14). Unfortunately, the Word of God that the Israelites depend on will not be realized, and they will be defeated, almost completely.

The prophecy of such a defeat can be found out in Zechariah 14:

> A day of the LORD is coming when your plunder will be divided among you. I will gather all the nations to Jerusalem to fight against it; the city will be captured, the houses ransacked, and the women raped. Half of the city will go into exile, but the rest of the people will not be taken from the city (Zechariah 14:1-2).

The Israelites will begin to weep. Their weeping has a double reason: the first is because of the pain of too great a defeat, and the other is because God gives them the spirit of repentance. Their mournful repentance is the same as that which their forefathers did on the Day of Atonement. At that time, the Day of Atonement that has been prophesized and practiced as service will finally be accomplished. Like their forefathers, they will thoroughly repent, and God will grant them mercy and forgiveness.

Let us read the Word of prophecy to be thus accomplished:

> And I will pour out on the house of David and the inhabitants of Jerusalem a spirit of grace and supplication. They will look on me, the one they have pierced, and they will mourn for him as one mourns for an only child, and grieve bitterly for him as one grieves for a firstborn son. On that day the weeping in Jerusalem will be great, like the weeping of Hadad Rimmon in the plain of Megiddo (Zechariah 12:10-11).

The repentance of the Israelites is concerning Jesus Christ. It is the repentance they need because of Jesus whom they hated so much as to cry out, "Crucify him!" Peter reminded the Israelites about this fact: you, with the help of wicked men, put him to death by the cross nailing him to (Acts 2:23). However, in the end, the Israelites will realize the fact that the very One whom they killed is the Messiah, for whom they have waited so long, and will be forgiven through Him.

At that time, in proportion to how they thoroughly repent, the fountain of thorough forgiveness will flow. On that day a fountain will be opened to the house of David and the inhabitants of Jerusalem, to cleanse them from sin and impurity (Zechariah 13:1). Is this the prophecy about the kind of fountain? It is the fountain of the saving blood to cleanse sin, whatever sin is, however evil sin is, or even the sin of idolatry (1 Peter 1:18-19). By this, the Day of Atonement will be completely fulfilled. The expression of this is in the diagram below:

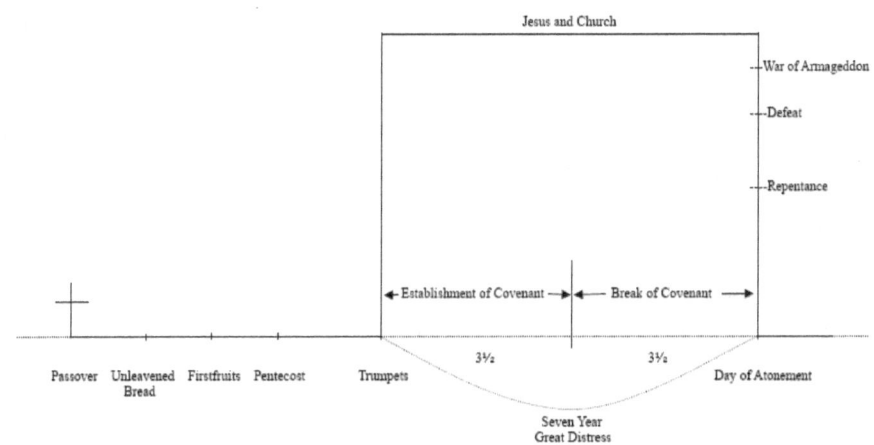

Chapter 11

The Tabernacles

The Festival of Tabernacles is the last of both the festivals of fall and the seven festivals of Israel. This festival is one of the three festivals that happen at the same time. Therefore, when they go to the temple to keep the Festival of Tabernacles, the Israelites cannot go with empty hands. They should go with tithes or offerings of thanksgiving. Also, the list of offerings they should offer to God at the Festival of Tabernacles is proposed, and they should go with offerings in accordance to this list (Numbers 29:13 ff).[1]

The Festival of Tabernacles is also called the Festival of Ingathering because it is a festival to reap and store the grains of fall. The Israelites finish their harvest and keep the festival with joy, which became the origin of Thanksgiving.[2] So the Festival of Ingathering is the festival called in direct relationship to the season of farming. At first, God also commanded the festival by this name through Moses: *Celebrate the Festival of Ingathering at the end of the year, when you gather in your crops from the field* (Exodus 23:16).

---

1. The case that presented the most offering to God on the Festival of Tabernacles was when Solomon offered a temple on the Festival of Tabernacles (1 Kings 8:2).

2. Epstein, *All about Jewish Holidays and Customs*, 29.

Whereas the Festival of Ingathering is a name related to farming, the Festival of Tabernacles emphasizes the life of the Israelites in their exodus from Egypt to their entering of Canaan. For forty years, they had no good places to stay in wilderness. They could only stay day by day in a tabernacle weaved of grass and sticks. For such a long time, God was responsible for the Israelites, laid them to sleep, fed them, and protected them. Remembering such a God, they called this festival the Festival of Tabernacles.[3]

The Festival of Tabernacles is **Succoth** in Hebrew, which means booth, hut, shed, or a temporal house. After Jacob returned from the house of his mother's brother, the first place he settled down was the very *Succoth*. The origin of the name is interesting: *Jacob, however, went to Succoth, where he built a place for himself and made shelters for his livestock. That is why the place is called Succoth* (Genesis 33:17). Jacob made his temporal place at Succoth.

When the Israelites came out of Egypt, the place where they were the first camped was *Succoth* (Exodus 12:27; Numbers 33:5). There they prepared a temporal place in a disorderly way and could only spend the night. Literally, the place was Succot, meaning booth. Like their forefather Jacob, they made a temporal booth and stayed there. This was the starting point of the Festival of Tabernacles. And the reason that the name became famous is the Festival of Tabernacles was called *Succoth* or *Succot*.[4]

Lesson of the Bible

How does the Bible teach about this festival called the Festival of Ingathering, or the Festival of Tabernacles, or *Succot?* Let us directly read the Word of God:

> The Lord said to Moses, Say to the Israelites: On the fifteenth day of the seventh month the Lord's Festival of Tabernacles begins, and it lasts for seven days. The first day is a sacred assembly; do no regular work. For seven days present offerings made to the Lord by fire, and on the eighth day hold a sacred assembly and

---

3. The Festival of Tabernacles is *hag ha Sukkot* (חג הסוכות) in Hebrew.

4. Kenneth A. Mathews, *Genesis 11:27-50:26, The American Commentary*, vol 2, ed, E. Ray Clendeney (Nashville, TN: Broadman & Holman Publishers, 2005).

present an offering made to the Lord by fire. It is the closing assembly; do no regular work... So beginning with the fifteenth day of the seventh month, after you have gathered the crops of the land, celebrate the festival to the Lord for seven days; the first day is a day of rest, and the eighth day also is a day of rest. On the first day you are to take choice fruit from the trees, and palm fronds, leafy branches and poplars, and rejoice before the Lord your God for seven days. Celebrate this as a festival to the Lord for seven days each year. This is to be a lasting ordinance for the generations to come; celebrate it in the seventh month. Live in booths for seven days: All native-born Israelites are to live in booths so your descendants will know that I had the Israelites live in booths when I brought them out of Egypt. I am the Lord your God. So Moses announced to the Israelites the appointed festivals of the Lord (Leviticus 23:33-36, 39-44).

The Festival of Tabernacles continues for a week beginning on *Tishr*, July 15th. So, the Festival of Tabernacles is started from the fifth day after the Day of Atonement. During the period of the Festival of Tabernacles, the Israelites do the following three things: (1) they live in a booth and are joyful before God (Leviticus 23:40); (2) they offer many offerings to God every day (Numbers 29:12-39); and (3) they publicly read the law. Let us explore these three things more specifically.

First, the Israelites gathered from all over the country and from all parts of the world and immediately built booths. They had to finish building by the 14th in order to participate in the Festival of Tabernacles that began on the next day. A number of booths were built on the streets of Jerusalem as well as on hills and fields. Of course, they were built within 1,000 cubits, which are about 500 meters, the distance one is able to walk on the Sabbath. Booths made by weaving a bunch of boughs reminded them of not only the poor life in the wilderness, but also of the protection of God during the period.[5]

Staying for a week in booths that they built, the Israelites endlessly rejoiced along with others:

Be joyful at your Festival—you, your sons and daughters, your menservants and maidservants, and the Levites, the aliens, the fa-

---

5. Glaser, *The Fall Festivals of Israel*, 161.

therless and the widows who live in your towns. For seven days celebrate the Festival to the Lord your God at the place the Lord will choose. For the Lord your God will bless you in all your harvest and in all the work of your hands, and your joy will be complete (Deuteronomy 16:14-15).

They were able to "take choice fruit from the trees, and palm fronds, leafy branches and poplars, and rejoice before the Lord your God for seven days" (Leviticus 23:40). They enjoyed abundant fruits, shake palm fronds, and rejoiced for seven days in the booths weaved of leafy branches and poplars. The Israelites were supposed to rejoice with the specifically anointed trees and fruits.[6]

Second, the Israelites were required to offer special offerings at the Festival of Tabernacles. Offerings presented for seven days were seventy bulls, seven goats daily, fourteen rams, and ninety-eight lambs. Additionally, fine flour of 33.6 ephah was added as a cereal offering.[7] The reason they presented seventy bulls as an offering was that they believed that the Gentile countries were seventy. According to Genesis 10, the descendents of Noah were seventy, and they spread all over the world in order to become the fathers of each nation. For their peace and well being, the bulls were sacrificed, and it was believed that some day those nations would acknowledge the God of Israel.[8]

In fact, according to the Word of God given to the Israelites, some day God would become the King who will reign over the Gentiles, and all peoples of the world will come to acknowledge that God is the only one God, as the Bible says, The Lord will be king over the whole earth. On that day there will be one Lord, and his name the only name (Zechariah 14:9).

---

6. However, rabbis interpret these four kinds of trees from various angles. "The product of goodly trees" stands for those who have knowledge of Torah and also have good deeds; "branches of palm trees" for those who have knowledge of Torah but have not good deeds; "boughs of leafy trees" for those who have good deeds but have not Torah; and "willows of the brook" for those who have not knowledge of torah or good deeds. Ibid., 193.

7. Because 1 ephah is 22 liters, it is 739 liters.

8. Williams, *The Holidays of God: Fall Festivals*, 23.

Third, the Israelites read the law every seven years on the Sabbatical Festival of Tabernacles:

> Then Moses commanded them: At the end of every seven years, in the year for canceling debts, during the Festival of Tabernacles, when all Israel comes to appear before the Lord your God at the place he will choose, you shall read this law before them in their hearing. Assemble the people—men, women and children, and the aliens living in your towns--so they can listen and learn to fear the Lord your God and follow carefully all the words of this law (Deuteronomy 31:10-13).

Accomplishment of the Past

Since the land of Israel was very dry, rain and water were extremely important. The Israelites associated the necessary rain with an event at the Festival of Tabernacles, which was a kind of prayer. The high priest took a golden pitcher to the Pool of Siloam and drew water from there. When he came into the Water Gate[9] with the golden bowl holding water of about one liter, a horn trumpet was blown three times. The priests then recited the words of Isaiah in one voice: *With joy you will draw water from the wells of salvation* (Isaiah 12:3).

When the high priest poured out the water into a silver pitcher in the south part of the altar of the burnt offering, the trumpet was blown three times again. A choir of Levites began to sing *Hallel* to the sound of the trumpet (Psalms 113-118). The congregation waved their palm branches and joined in singing, *Save now, I pray, O Lord; O Lord, I pray, send now prosperity* (Psalms 118:25). With this singing, the priests with palm branches in hand, marched around the altar. While the priest slowly poured the water, singing continued, and congregation continued to wave palm branches.[10]

Easily seen is that this event of pouring the water was accomplished through Jesus Christ. To begin with, when Jesus Christ rode a donkey into Jerusalem and entered the temple, the people

---

9. Originally, this gate was the southern gate of Jerusalem but because of this service, it was called the Water Gate. Howard & Rosenthal, *The Festivals of the Lord*, 138.

10. Ibid., 139.

shouted, *Hosanna! Blessed is he who comes in the name of the Lord! Blessed is the King of Israel!* (John 12:13). Hosanna means to "save us!" So the Israelites shouted the sound, when the high priest was pouring out the water of salvation, symbolizing Jesus Christ.

If so, is He the water of salvation? Yes, Jesus Christ is the water of salvation. To tell us that He is the water of the Festival of Tabernacles we have his own Word:

> On the last and greatest day of the Festival, Jesus stood and said in a loud voice, If anyone is thirsty, let him come to me and drink. Whoever believes in me, as the Scripture has said, streams of living water will flow from within him (John 7:37-38).

The water that the high priest drew from the Pool of Siloam could never solve the spiritual thirst of the Israelites. The water was poured out and thus had to be drawn again, and it was poured out again. To the Israelites who had such a thirst, Jesus said, *By this he meant the Spirit, whom those who believed in him were later to receive. Up to that time the Spirit had not been given, since Jesus had not yet been glorified* (John 7:39).

Jesus Christ invited the Israelites to drink living water during the Festival of Tabernacles. Although the high priest daily poured out the water, none of them experienced satisfaction thus far. To such thirsty people, Jesus proposed "streams of living water." The streams of living water would give them joy because they repented at the Festival of Tabernacles and realized the meaning of atonement. Likewise, all they have to do in order the joy of transformation is to repent and accept Jesus Christ, the protagonist of atonement.[11]

Although the celebration of the water at the Festival of Tabernacles was important, it was not everything. The celebration to shed light on the temple was also important. From the evening of the following day to the last day of the Festival of Tabernacles, the Israelites inaugurated the service to lighten the temple. Lighting four lamp-stands of fifty cubits high in the center of the court

---

11. This process can be summarized into repentance, redemption, and rejoicing. As a result, the three festivals of fall is the gospel to beautifully tell the order of salvation.

would make the temple brighter, similar to daytime. The members of the Sanhedrin, pious people, and people of each sect danced to the music and to the sound of praise until late night. The song they sang was Psalms 120-134.[12]

The light made the temple and Jerusalem brighter, but as a result, none of the Israelites were enlightened physically or morally. At that very time, Jesus Christ said, *I am the light of the world. Whoever follows me will never walk in darkness, but will have the light of life* (John 8:12). As a proof of this word, He shed light on a woman who lived morally in the dark. He gave the light of life to the woman caught in the act of adultery (John 8:2-11).

This was not all! On the evening of that day, Jesus Christ met a blind man coming out of the temple. The blind man attended the Festival of Tabernacles there in a numerous time. However, he was still blind. Jesus said, *While I am in the world, I am the light of the world* (John 9:5). As if he proved his saying, he told the blind man to wash in the Pool of Siloam, and the moment he obeyed, the man was able to see. The light of the Festival of Tabernacles could not make him see, but Jesus, the true light made him see.

The last day of the Festival of Tabernacles was the climax of the festival. For six days they blew the trumpet three times every day. On the last day of the Festival of Tabernacles, the horn was blown seven times, and the blowing was repeated three times. So, they blew it twenty one times altogether. Also, while the priests walked around the altar of the burnt offering only once for the first six days, on the last day they walked around seven times. Walking around the altar, they shouted hosanna (Psalms 118:25), and the people waved palm branches.[13]

The priests and the people blew the trumpet and circled the altar, but did these services give them joy in a true sense? Of course not! Such celebrations were only annual activities; what was necessary for them was relationship with the Savior and the Holy Spirit. On the last day of the festival, Jesus Christ demonstrated that He Himself is the Savior and promised the Holy Spirit: *If anyone is thirsty, let him come to me and drink* (John 7:37). At long last, Jesus Christ

---

12. Ibid., 140.
13. Ibid., 141.

became the living water and the light Who responded to the prayers that many people prayed on the Festival of Tabernacles.

Practice in the Present

The most outstanding symbol in the Festival of Tabernacles was a booth. Therefore, as soon as the Day of Atonement ended, the Israelites built a booth in the courtyard or on the roof. The booth was required to be high enough for a tall person to enter and wide enough to set a table in. The booth had three walls, and one of them was curtained. The roof was made with branches, which were sparse enough to allow the stars to be seen and to allow the drops of rain to enter. Also, it had to block sunlight during the day. Then it was beautifully decorated by various methods.[14]

On the Festival of Tabernacles, the Israelites waved the fruit of goodly trees with their left hand and held three kinds of other branches with the right. They could not wave the branches in the right hand. A branch of palm trees was to be placed in the middle of the hand, and two willows and three boughs of leafy trees were to be placed on the right and left sides, respectively. So they waved a branch of palm trees in the left hand and held three kinds of branches in the right every morning at the synagogue.[15]

They could not wave the branches just any old way, either. First, they had to stand facing east and wave the branches slowly and carefully three times. Then, they were waving branches to the south, then to the west, and then to the north up and down three times, respectively. To wave toward the four directions was to acknowledge the fact that the four directions belong to God, and to wave up and down was to express that heaven and earth also belong to God.[16]

The Israelites returned from the synagogue to booths once again. Upon entering the booths, the father said the following blessing: "Blessed art Thou, O Lord our God, King of the universe, who has sanctified us with Thy commandments and commanded us to dwell

---

14. Howard & Rosenthal, *The Festivals of the Lord*, 143.
15. Glaser, *The Fall Festivals of Israel*, 194.
16. Ibid.

in a booth."[17] Once they entered the booths, the family members took a few moments to reflect on the meaning and nature of the booth that would become their temporal home during this festival. This reflection included the following content.[18]

> Do not say in your heart, "My own power and the might of my own hand have won this wealth for me" (Deuteronomy 8:17); you should remember the Lord your God, as it is He who gives you strength to make progress. Therefore, the people leave [their] houses, which are full of everything good at the season of ingathering, and dwell in booths, as a reminder of those who had no possessions in the wilderness and no houses in which to live. For this reason, the Holy One established the festival of Tabernacles at the time of the ingathering from the threshing floor and the wine press, that the people should not be proud of their well-furnished houses.

Then the Israelites had the table fellowship, sharing the meal. After the meal was over, they sang the songs of the festival and slept in their booths. If it rained more than two hours, one person had to pray, eat a small piece of bread about the size of an olive in the booth, and go back to the house. If one of the family members was ill, from the beginning, he or she was to sleep in the house, not in the booth. They spent every day in this way during the Festival of Tabernacles. In the daytime, they visited others' booths and spoke of the beauty of their booths.[19]

The last and seventh day of the Festival of Tabernacles was the "Great Hosanna."[20] The congregation of Israel circled the synagogue every day, waving the branches and shouting hosanna. On that last day, however, the entire congregation circled the synagogue seven times, with more branches, shouting hosanna. To circle seven times was to remember the religious fact that the priests circled the altar of the burnt offering and the historical fact that they circled seven times in order to destroy Jericho.

---

17. Ibid., 195.
18. Ibid., 196.
19. Ibid., 197-8.
20. It is *Hoshana Rabbah* in Hebrew.

The eighth day of the Festival of Tabernacles was regarded not only as the day to complete the Festival of Tabernacles, but also as the beginning of the festival to start a new farming season.[21] In the minds of the Israelites, the day was an act of prolonging the event one more day because they wanted a deeper fellowship with God. The important service of the day included a prayer for abundant rain in New Year. Also, reading especially Ecclesiastes, they reflected on all things and they were reminded of all things including the Festival of Tabernacles meaningless. This service helped to moderate the excessive exultation they did during the Festival of Tabernacles.[22]

Fulfillment of the Future

As mentioned in the previous chapter, the Festival of Trumpets, the Day of Atonement, and the Festival of Tabernacles are the festivals of fall as well as the last festivals of a year. These festivals imply the eschatology that is indispensible to Christianity. The Festival of Trumpets implies the Second Advent of Jesus Christ in the air and the rapture of the Church, the Day of Atonement implies the national repentance of the Israelites, and the Festival of Tabernacles implies the events that will occur after the Festival of Trumpets and the Day of Atonement.

The national repentance of the Israelites will occur after much cruel oppression and defeat. And yet, without God's grace, they will not be able to go through. As God prophesized through Daniel, God will pour out tremendous grace at a designated time. Let us read the prophecy of Daniel again: *Know and understand this: From the issuing of the decree to restore and rebuild Jerusalem until the Anointed One, the ruler, comes, there will be seven 'sevens,' and sixty-two 'sevens'...* (Daniel 9:25).

Artaxerxes, the king commanded Nehemiah to rebuild the city (Nehemiah 2:1-8), twenty years after his enthronement (464 B.C.). It was then 465 B.C. Then, it was prophesized that the Anointed One would be killed after seven sevens and sixty-two sevens, in

---

21. It is *Shemii Atzeret* in Hebrew.
22. Ibid., 199-200.

other words, sixty-nine sevens (Daniel 9:26). In other words, 483 years after the commandment, Christ was crucified on the cross. It was A.D. 30.[23] And, after Christ was crucified on the cross, the era of the Church started.

When he Church is raptured at long last and the era of the Church is over, the tribulation of seven years begins, and the seven years become the seventieth week. So if the era of the Church does not exist, the prophecy of Daniel jumps over the era of the Church and directly connects the death of Jesus Christ with the great tribulation of seven years. In the end of the seven year great tribulation, by God's interruption, the Israelites repent nationally and accept Jesus Christ as their Messiah whom they crucified on the cross. At the moment that the tribulation ends, Jesus Christ will come on earth together with believers. From that time forward, the Festival of Tabernacles will start.

Let us read directly the prophecy of the Bible:

> Then the Lord will go out and fight against those nations, as he fights in the day of battle. On that day his feet will stand on the Mount of Olives, east of Jerusalem, and the Mount of Olives will be split in two from east to west, forming a great valley, with half of the mountain moving north and half moving south... On that day living water will flow out from Jerusalem, half to the eastern sea and half to the western sea, in summer and in winter. The Lord will be king over the whole earth. On that day there will be one Lord, and his name the only name (Zechariah 14:3-4, 8-9).

The Lord will defeat the armies of the nations who attack Israel and He will stand on the Mount of Olives. The living water that Jesus Christ promised will come up from Jerusalem and wet the whole world. He will become the King over the whole earth and reign over the world. Also, the nations will come to Jerusalem in order to keep the Festival of Tabernacles: *Then the survivors from all the nations that have attacked Jerusalem will go up year after year to worship the King, the Lord Almighty, and to celebrate the Festival of Tabernacles* (Zechariah 14:16).

---

23. Tim LaHaye, ed., *Prophecy Study Bible* (Chattanooga, TN: AMG Publishers, 2000), 911-12.

The Festival of Tabernacles that Israel as well as other nations keep means the introduction of the Kingdom of a Thousand Years. As the King of the Kings, Jesus Christ and Christians, as the kings, will reign over the world. He will finally sit on the throne of David. Satan who defied Christ and the Church will be cast into the Abyss for a thousand years (Revelation 20:1-2). During that time, the temple that the Israelites long dreamed about, will be rebuilt (Ezekiel 40 ff).

The Israelites were originally given the precious name of the nation of priests, which included the commandment to spread God's love and power all over the world (Exodus 19:4-6). However, the Israelites did not exert the commandment, and rather disdained the people of God. As a result, Israel's privilege to exert the commandment was given to the Gentile Church.[24] However, during the Kingdom of a Thousand Years, the Israelites will again have the opportunity to exercise that privilege.

As soon as the Kingdom of a Thousand Years is completed, as the Bible foretells, Satan will be temporally released (Revelation 20:3). Satan will entice the people of all four directions and arouse the final war against the believers of Jesus Christ. The nations mainly recruited at that time will be Gog and Magog (Revelation 20:8; Ezekiel 38-39). God will cast them into hell by the final judgment so they will receive the eternal judgment there (Revelation 20:9-10). God will also judge all resurrected unbelievers from His judgment seat of the white throne. They will be judged by their acts and cast into hell (Revelation 20:13-14).

In contrast, all people who accepted Jesus Christ as their Savior will be led to a new heaven and a new earth because the first heaven and the first earth will have passed away (2 Peter 3:12). There, they will eternally live with God. With gloriously changed appearances, they will spend the Festival of Tabernacles, doing the following two things: first, they will worship and glorify God; second,

---

24. Seong Cheol Hong, *Junimui Jisangmyeongreong: Seonggyeongjeok Uimiwa Jeokyong* (*The Lord's Great Commandment: Its Biblical Meaning and Application*), 157 ff.

they will eternally live, endlessly enjoying God's glorious presence.[25]

To illustrate the above in a diagram, is as follows:

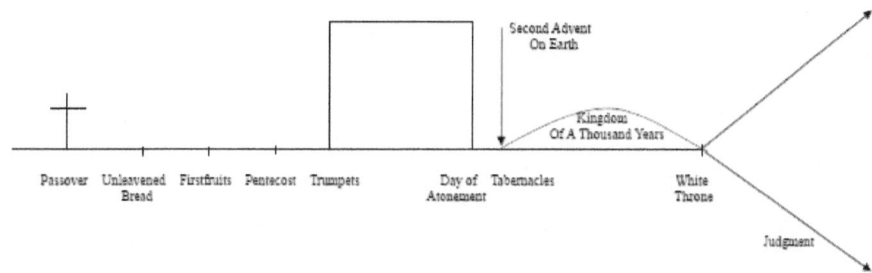

---

25. Philip G. Ryken, *The Message of Salvation* (Downers Grove, IL: InterVarsity Press, 2001), 275 ff.

Conclusion

For now, the journey through the seven festivals presented in Leviticus 23 is finished. The journey may have been short or long. Through this journey, we investigated, in order, the Festival of Passover, the Festival of Unleavened Bread, the Festival of First Fruits, the Festival of Pentecost, the Festival of Trumpets, the Day of Atonement, and the Festival of Tabernacles. In a cycle of the twelve months of a year, these festivals were enough to occasionally play a role of shelter, more so for the Israelites, who gained a rest at every festival physically and spiritually.

We investigated how the Israelites gained rest physically and spiritually, from the shelter. In order to learn the shelter of the Israelites, we have studied the background of the Old Testament, what they believe, which is still practiced, and how it was historically accomplished. Furthermore, we have also studied the relationship between the shelter and the agricultural products.

However, we cannot stay only there. The reason is simple! Since all Scriptures, whether they be the Old Testament or the New Testament, were recorded by the inspiration of the Holy Spirit (2 Timothy 3:15-16; 2 Peter 1:21). The study of the Old Testament needs the solution of the New Testament, and the study of the New Testament needs the questions of the Old Testament. In other words, the Old Testament should be approached from the perspective of the New Testament and vice versa.

For this reason, as we are going through a journey of Leviticus 23, we could only approach the implications of each festival or, each shelter from the perspective of the New Testament. In fact, such an approach is a basic attitude of Bible studies, and at the same time, it provided us with great discovery and joy. What was uncovered in this way is the fact that the three festival seasons of Israel are also those of Christianity.

We have discovered together the fact that the three festival seasons recorded in the Old Testament--the Festival of Passover, Pentecost, and the Festival of Tabernacles--imply the First Coming of Jesus Christ, the Coming of the Holy Spirit, and the Second Coming of Jesus Christ, respectively. We have also discovered the fact that the seven festivals expanded in Leviticus 23, can be applied to the seven historical events of Christianity. As repeatedly mentioned above, the seven festivals were also already included in the three festival seasons.

The Passover was the important festival that includes both the Festival of Unleavened Bread and the Festival of the First Fruits. Putting these three festivals together is called the Festival of Unleavened Bread or the Festival of Passover (Exodus 23:15; Deuteronomy 16:1). This festival was fulfilled through the First Coming of Jesus Christ in the New Testament, which became the most significant event in Christianity not only because the climax of the fulfillment is the very death and resurrection of Jesus, but also because His death and resurrection are the core of the gospel.

In addition, the Festival of Passover when lambs were killed was fulfilled by the death of Jesus Christ, the Festival of Unleavened Bread by the burial of Jesus, and the Festival of the First Fruits by the resurrection of Christ. This death and resurrection of Jesus Christ became the core of the gospel because His death was the redemptive death for sinners, and His resurrection became the way that all believers who accepted such redemptive death could become righteous (Romans 4:25).

This is why the festivals of spring (the Festival of Passover, the Festival of Unleavened Bread, and the Festival of First Fruits) were presented in one category. Jesus Christ died on the cross (the Festival of Passover), was buried (the Festival of Unleavened Bread), and arose on the third day after He died (the Festival of First Fruits). What a wonderful fulfillment! After the Coming of the Holy Spirit, the word of the Apostle Peter who first proclaimed the gospel held the same message, as follows: ... You killed the author of life, but God raised him from the dead. We are witnesses of this (Acts 3:14-15).

The Apostle Paul, who best arranged the content of the gospel, also proclaimed the same. Here is Paul's proclamation:

> Now, brothers, I want to remind you of the gospel I preached to you, which you received and on which you have taken your stand... For what I received I passed on to you as of first importance: that Christ died for our sins according to the Scriptures, that he was buried, that he was raised on the third day according to the Scriptures (1 Corinthians 15:1, 3-4).

The words above also very clearly include the three festival seasons. "That Christ died for our sins according to the Scriptures" is a clear representation of the Passover as in the prophecy and modeled in the Old Testament. Just as the lamb of Passover died on behalf of the Israelites, Jesus Christ died on the cross on behalf of all sinners. The death on the cross is the most important historical event in Christianity because unless He died, nobody could solve the problem of sin.

Then "that he was buried," needless to say, is also the fulfillment of the Festival of Unleavened Bread. Just as the Israelites could come out of Egypt through the work of Passover, sinners can come out of sin through Jesus' death. Just as the Israelites ate unleavened bread remembering that they should endure suffering in Egypt, so, after He died on the cross, Jesus Christ became a tasteless body and was buried in a tomb.

Finally, "that he was raised on the third day according to the Scriptures" is the Festival of the First Fruits. Just as the Israelites offered the first fruits, wavering it before God, so Jesus Christ became the First Fruits by living again. If it were not for His resurrection, nobody would have life that could resemble the image of Christ because the Lord of resurrection provides the believers with the direction and power of life.

As a result, the fact that the three festivals of spring are not only for the Israelites became clear. The festivals teach that all peoples in the world should come before Jesus Christ. This is the festival of invitation to solve the problems of sin and death through Jesus Christ who died on the cross and has lived again. Just as the Israelites could come out of Egypt through the festivals of spring, we should accept the fact that the death and resurrection of Jesus Christ are the redemptive death and resurrection for each of us.

The festivals of spring do not teach only that! They also teach that those who solved the problems of sin and death through Jesus Christ all should spread the gospel. Just as God, through Moses, commanded the Israelites to keep the festivals of spring, so God commands all believers to spread the good news about Jesus Christ, the content of the gospel. Whether a believer is a pastor or a lay person, he or she should spread the gospel proclaimed in the Old Testament and in the New Testament.

The second important festival to the Israelites was Pentecost. For them, Pentecost is the festival to keep on the fiftieth day from the day that they brought the First Fruits. Likewise, the Pentecost is also very important in the New Testament and in Christianity. Jesus Christ showed His resurrected body to His disciples. He appeared ten times in forty days. After the fortieth day, He ascended before His disciples and went to live beside God.

Ten days later, Jesus Christ received the Holy Spirit from God the Father and sent the Spirit to the believers of 120 as a gift (Acts 2:33), on exactly the fiftieth day after the resurrection of Christ. The Holy Spirit, who came on that day, filled the 120 believers with His Presence. In a strict sense, it is also true that the Church was created by the coming of the Holy Spirit and thus it started the Era of the Church. However, above all, we should look at the changed lives of the 120 believers.

Although they believed in Jesus Christ as their Lord and followed him, their lives had not yet changed. Almost nothing had changed expect for the fact that they were the disciples of Jesus Christ. They were afraid of persecution from all of their surroundings. In order to escape persecution, they abandoned their Lord, denied Him, and even ran away. On top of that, as witnesses of Jesus Christ, they frequently desecrated His name!

However, the Holy Spirit changed all things. On receiving the Holy Spirit, they, above all, became audaciously adventurous. They began to live the lives of unprecedented change. Not only this, but the power also began to appear in them. Although the 120 were a little group, like a hand of dust before the enormous Roman

Empire, they audaciously began to spread the gospel before the Empire. And, finally, they pulled down the Empire with the gospel.

The infilling of the Holy Spirit that the early Christians experienced is a great challenge to us Christians of the twenty first century. Unless we experience the infilling of the Holy Spirit, we cannot win this threatening generation to Jesus Christ. So, how can we experience the filling of the Holy Spirit like the early Christians? The methods are also described in the Bible. If we do what the 120 did, it is possible. They did the following three things.

First, they unconditionally obeyed the commandment of the Lord. The Lord commanded them not to leave Jerusalem and to wait (Acts 1:4). The believers of 120 absolutely followed the commandment. It is the same for us! The Lord gives commandments to each of us. Whatever they are, we should obey. The commandments that the Lord gives us, upon further acquaintance, are for us. Although we may not understand at first, if we obey as the commandments are given, we will be filled with the Holy Spirit.

By the way, God does not give the same commandments to His children. To a child, God gives the commandment that he or she can follow. For example, it is like reading the Bible daily, praying, evangelizing, being faithful to worship, offering perfect tithes, and so on. To grown children, God gives the greater commandments; for example, praying for and loving one's enemy, sparing time for serving, engaging more in missions, and so on. Whatever the commandment is, when we obey it, we can be filled with the Holy Spirit.

Second, they engaged in praying together (Acts 1:14). First, the 120 believers prayed with one mind. They were to pray only. How can it be said so? They engaged in praying for ten days and experienced the fullness of the Holy Spirit. Likewise, in order to be filled with the Holy Spirit, we should also be of one mind. And we should be hard pressed to pray. How long should we pray? We should pray until God responds. God wants to respond to the prayers of His children. The heavenly Father, above all, promised to give the Holy Spirit as a gift to those who ask: *How much more will your Father in heaven give the Holy Spirit to those who ask him* (Luke 11:13). Of course, this promise is the Word of Jesus who responds to all prayers.

Third, the 120 believers gave up their individual ambition and desire. According to Acts 1:26, when they selected Matthias instead of Iscariot Judah, they innocently selected him by casting lots. None of them used their privileges. Neither Peter, the head disciple of Jesus; James, the leader of the early church; nor Maria, the mother of Jesus, used their privileges. Giving up their privileges, they asked only for God's will. For this reason, they were filled with the Holy Spirit as a gift.

This is the same for us! When we give up our individual wills and ask for God's will, we can be filled with the Holy Spirit. In order to exert privilege, we should not use the authority. In order to reach a status, we should not organize a political group. Furthermore, we should not cause intrigue against others. We should never abuse money or a court, either. Although we can attain our purpose through these ways, **we would never experience the fullness of the Holy Spirit that the Lord promised.**

The Israelites also kept the festivals of fall—the Festival of Trumpets, The Day of Atonement, and the Festival of Tabernacles—regarding them as important. As mentioned above, by putting these three festivals of fall together, they can be dealt with as the third festival of Israel. We have already studied that the fall festival is called the Festival of Tabernacles or the Festival of Ingathering. The Israelites kept the festival of fall in the temple after finishing the last farming of each year.

In Christianity, the Festival of Tabernacles, as the third important festival, designates the Second Advent of the Lord. At the end of the world, the Lord will appear in the air with the trumpet blast, and, at that moment, all born again Christians will be raptured into the air to meet the Lord. This is the fulfillment of the Festival of Trumpets. During the period, the Israelites will come to repent. From that time on, the Israelites will be engaged in evangelism and missions for the evangelization of the world. This is the fulfillment of the Day of Atonement.

This is the beginning of the Kingdom of a Thousand Years. For a thousand years, Satan and the angels who follow Satan will be imprisoned in the Abyss. The peoples in the world will gather at the temple to observe the Festival of Tabernacles. At last, God will receive worship and praise from all peoples. Of course, born again

Christians will be changed to be like Christ in order to play a role of kings along with Christ. So, the Festival of Tabernacles is the completion of all festivals.

As a result, the three festival seasons of Israel are the same as those of Christianity. The three festival seasons, that is, the Passover, the Pentecost, and the Festival of Tabernacles all designate the First and Second Comings of Jesus Christ, and the Coming of the Holy Spirit. Interestingly, the Pentecost, that is the festival of early summer, is placed between the First Coming and the Second Coming of Jesus Christ. The Pentecost, that is the advent of the Holy Spirit, is an important link in connecting the Cross of the past and the Second Coming of the future.

These three festival seasons are very suggestive to us. The First Coming of Jesus including the event of the cross, teaches the fact that all people should be born again. Also, the Coming of the Holy Spirit teaches the experience of holiness for all believers to receive when they are filled with the Holy Spirit. Finally, the Second Coming of Jesus teaches the serious fact that all believers should be ready to meet the Lord, because the Lord will come again and bring believers to account for how each of us lived our lives.

Index

Genesis
1:27, 118
2:2, 34
2:2-3, 27
3:32, 118
4:1-2, 118
4:8, 118
8:1, 118
12:3, 117
15:6, 117
21:2, 118
22:2, 58
22:3, 118
22:9, 58
22:9-10, 119
22:14, 58
22:17-18, 117
23:1-2, 118
25:21, 118
33:17, 142
41:39-44, 118
49:31, 118

Exodus
1:12-14, 39
2:23-25, 39
4:22, 40
5:1, 39
5:2, 39
6:6-7, 46
9:14-16, 40
12:1-14, 41
12:2, 21, 54
12:3, 54
12:6, 54
12:8-9, 60
12:12, 44
12:12-13, 84
12:12-20, 66
12:13, 44
12:14, 44
12:14-20, 66
12:15, 67, 68
12:16, 66
12:18, 67
12:19, 68
12:22, 42
12:26, 46
12:27, 142
12:30, 43
12:34, 45
12:42, 68
12:46, 42, 54, 60
13:4, 22
13:6-8, 66
13:7, 67
13:10, 45
16:22, 34
16:22, 26–27
16:23, 31
16:29, 34
16:36, 88
19:1, 11, 103
19:4-6, 152
19:18-20, 120
19:19, 115
20:8, 34
20:8-11, 25, 27
20:18-20, 108
22:27, 142
22:29, 84
23:12, 30
23:13, 30
23:14-17, 7, 19, 99
23:15, 66, 156
23:16, 97, 141
23:19, 84
25:22, 12
30:11-16, 57
31:15-17, 30
32:22, 99
32:28, 107
34:18, 66
34:19, 84
34:21, 31
34:22, 88
35:2, 30
35:3, 31
40:34-38, 12

Leviticus
2:11, 100
16:3-10, 128
16:5, 130

163

16:12-16, 128
16:21-22, 128
16:31, 131
17:11, 135
22:22-24, 42
23:1-2, 13, 17
23:1-44, 13-16
23:2, 13
23:3, 13, 25
23:4, 13, 25, 39
23:5, 13, 39
23:6, 66
23:6-8, 14, 63
23:7-8, 14, 26, 56, 66
23:8, 14
23:9, 14, 17
23:9-14, 76
23:10, 14, 88
23:11, 14, 26, 75, 88
23:12, 14, 88
23:14, 76
23:15, 63, 88
23:15-16, 26, 87, 89, 97
23:15-21, 99
23:17, 105
23:23, 17
23:23-25, 15, 112
23:24, 26
23:26-32, 15, 125
23:29, 126
23:30, 126
23:31-32, 26
23:32, 126
23:33, 17
23:33-36, 143
23:35-36, 26
23:38, 25
23:39-44, 143
23:40, 143, 144

25:9-10, 114

Numbers
10:1-10, 114
15:17-21, 34
15:32, 30, 31
15:36, 30
19:9, 127
28:3-8, 65
28:19-24, 65
28:25, 66
28:26, 98
28:26-31, 99
29:1-5, 115
29:7-11, 132
29:8-11, 127
29:12-39, 143
29:13, 141
33:3, 64
33:5, 142

Deuteronomy
5:12-15, 28
6:23, 11
8:8, 84
8:17, 149
15:19-16:17, 103
16:1, 156
16:1-17, 21
16:2, 45, 65
16:3, 42, 64, 66
16:4, 67
16:5-6, 57
16:6, 58
16:7-8, 67
16:8, 66
16:9-12, 99
16:11, 100
16:14-15, 144
16:16, 58, 99
18:1, 77
18:3-4, 77

26:1-2, 77
26:3, 77, 80
26:4, 77
26:5, 81
26:5-10, 78
26:9-10, 81
31:10-12, 145
31:10-13, 145

Joshua
5:10-11, 44
6:20, 115

Ruth
4:21-22, 105

1 Samuel
1:11, 118
1:17, 118
6:19, 134

1 Kings
6:1, 22
6:38, 22
8:2, 22, 141

1 Chronicles
21:16-17, 58
21:18, 58
2 Chronicles
3:1, 58
8:13, 99

Nehemiah
1:1, 22
2:1-8, 150
2:1, 22
6:15, 22
13:31, 31

Esther
2:16, 22

3:7, 22
8:9, 22

Psalms
1:1-6, 93
11:1-7, 93
15:1-5, 93
19:7-14, 93
22:16-18, 70
25:4-10, 93
30:1, 101
33:1-12, 117
63:1-8, 93
67:1-7, 93
68:7-10, 105
78:1-72, 93, 94
91:5-6, 35
93:1-5, 94
94:12-23, 94
95:1-7, 94
96:1-13, 94
98:1-9, 94
99:1-9, 94
103:1-22, 94
103:12, 68
105:1-11, 94
106:1-5, 94
111:1-10, 94
112:1-10, 94
113-118, 145
115-118, 47
118:5-9, 117
118:25,145, 147
119:1-176, 93
120-134, 147
128:1-6, 94
130:1-8, 94
138:1-8, 94
148:1-14, 94
150:1, 80
150:1-6, 94
150:6, 94

Proverbs
31:10, 33
31:27-29, 33

Isaiah
1:18, 130
11:9, 117
12:3, 145
27:13, 115
52:14, 70
53:5, 53, 71
53:6-7, 53
53:7, 53
57:14-58:14, 132

Jeremiah
2:3, 83
17:21-22, 31
31:33, 107

Ezekiel
1:4,104
3:12, 104
36:26-28, 108

Daniel
7:25, 137
9:25, 150
9:26, 151
9:27, 137
12:7, 137

Joel
2:31-32, 137

Amos
8:5, 31

Micah
7:18-20, 117
7:19, 117n

Habakkuk
3:13, 104
3:15-16, 104
3:18, 104

Zechariah
1:7, 22
7:2-5, 126
8:19, 126
9:9, 55
9:14, 115, 120
12:2-4, 138
12:6,138
12:10, 70
12:10-11, 139
13:1, 139
14:1-2, 138
14:3-4, 151
14:8-9, 151
14:9, 144
14:16, 151

Malachi
1:8, 42

Matthew
28:1,83
22:34, 55
22:46, 55
24:14, 109
24:21,122, 137
24:22,137
26:23, 52
26:26, 49
26:26-28, 49
26:28, 48
27:52-53, 85
26:57, 56
27:22, 59
27:51,135
27:59-60, 70
28:1, 83

28:19, 92
28:19-20, 109

Mark
15:1, 56
15:25, 55
15:33, 56
15:34, 56
15:37, 56
15:42-43, 83
16:15, 109

Luke
3:23, 52
11:13, 159
22:8, 48
22:19, 48, 72
22:20, 48
22:44, 56
23:6, 56
23:24, 56
23:26, 56
23:41, 52
23:45, 135
24:25, 9
24:27, 9
24:49, 91, 92, 106

John
1:29, 51, 53, 61
2:16, 59
2:19, 59, 61
5:14, 36
5:16, 35
5:17, 36
5:21, 37
5:22, 37
5:29, 82
5:39, 9
6:29, 82
6:32-33, 61
6:47, 60

6:53-55, 60
6:53-57, 71
6:54, 60
7:19, 36
7:21, 36
7:37, 147
7:37-38, 146
7:39, 146
8:2-11, 147
8:12, 147
9:3-4, 36
9:5, 147
9:41, 37
12:1, 54
12:12, 54
12:13, 146
16:8-11, 106
16:13, 106
18:12, 56
18:13, 56
18:28, 53
19:4, 52, 55
19:31, 56
19:31-36, 61
19:32-34, 70
19:36, 54
20:21, 91
20:22, 91
24:49, 106

Acts
1:4, 92, 109, 159
1:5, 91
1:8, 92, 106, 109
1:14, 91, 159
1:16, 91
1:26, 160
2:2-4, 108
2:4, 91
2:9-11, 106
2:13, 106
2:17, 111
2:23, 139

2:32-33, 90
2:33, 106, 158
2:37-38, 106
2:41, 106
3:14-15, 157
4:4, 106
4:31, 107
20:7, 37

Romans
1:4, 52, 81
3:25-26, 134
4:25, 52, 83, 156
8:11, 107
8:14, 107
8:23, 86
11:16, 85
14:12, 123
16:5, 85

1 Corinthians
3:12-15, 122
5:7-8, 61, 72
11:24, 72
15:1, 157
15:3-4, 157
15:20, 81
15:23-24, 82
15:51-52, 121
15:53, 121
16:2, 37
16:15-16, 85

2 Corinthians
3:6, 107
3:16-17, 107
5:10, 123

Ephesians
1:13, 106
1:14, 86
2:8, 111

5:18, 107
5:26-27, 123

1 Thessalonians
4:13-17, 122

2 Thessalonians
2:3-4, 138
2:7, 122

2 Timothy
3:15-16, 13, 155

Hebrews
4:15, 52
5:8-9, 120
9:5, 134
9:12, 53

7:26, 52
9:12-14, 135
11:19, 120

James
1:18, 85

1 Peter
1:18-19, 139
1:23, 85

2 Peter
1:21, 13, 155
3:12, 152

1 John
2:2, 136
3:2, 107, 121

Revelation

1:5-6, 57
1:7, 70
1:10, 38
1:14, 123
5:9, 62
7:9-10, 57
12:14, 137
14:4, 86
16:14, 138
16:16, 138
19:6-8, 123
20:1-2, 152
20:3, 152
20:8, 152
20:9-10, 152
20:13-14, 152

www.ingramcontent.com/pod-product-compliance
Lightning Source LLC
Chambersburg PA
CBHW021144230426
43667CB00005B/244